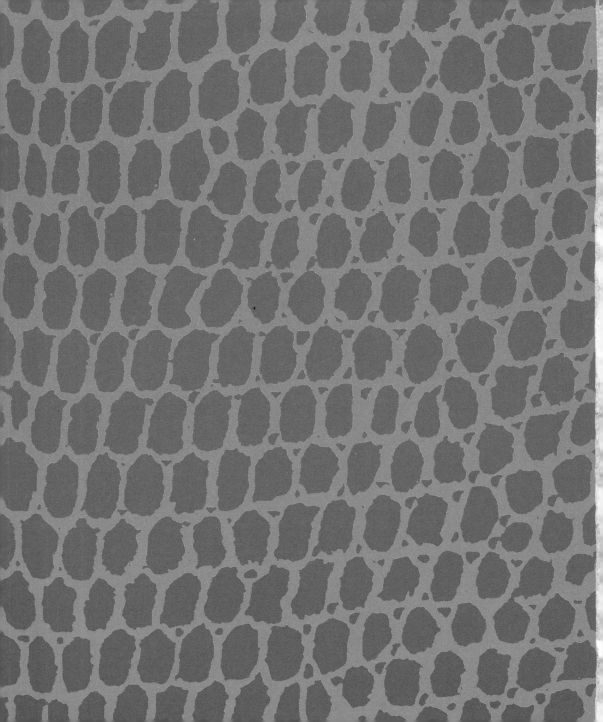

Animal Planet

Saltwater Aquarium Problem Solver

JEFF KURTZ

Saltwater Aquarium Problem Solver

Project Team
Editors: Craig Sernotti, David E. Boruchowitz
Copy Editor: Joann Woy
Indexer: Joann Woy
Design Concept: Leah Lococo Ltd., Stephanie Krautheim
Design Layout: Patricia Escabi

T.F.H. Publications
President/CEO: Glen S. Axelrod
Executive Vice President: Mark E. Johnson
Publisher: Christopher T. Reggio
Production Manager: Kathy Bontz

Discovery Communications, Inc. Book Development Team
Marjorie Kaplan, President, Animal Planet Media
Carol LeBlanc, Vice President, Licensing
Elizabeth Bakacs, Vice President, Creative Services
Brigid Ferraro, Director, Licensing
Peggy Ang, Vice President, Animal Planet Marketing
Caitlin Erb, Manager, Licensing

T.F.H. Publications, Inc.
One TFH Plaza
Third and Union Avenues
Neptune City, NJ 07753

Printed and bound in China
08 09 10 11 12 1 3 5 7 9 8 6 4 2

Library of Congress Cataloging-in-Publication Data
Kurtz, Jeffrey.
 Saltwater aquarium problem solver / Jeff Kurtz.
   p. cm. — (Animal Planet pet care library)
 Includes index.
 ISBN 978-0-7938-3796-0 (alk. paper)
 1. Marine aquariums. I. Animal Planet (Television network) II. Title.
 SF457.1.K86 2008
 639.34'2—dc22

                              2007042901

This book has been published with the intent to provide accurate and authoritative information in regard to the subject matter within. While every reasonable precaution has been taken in preparation of this book, the author and publisher expressly disclaim responsibility for any errors, omissions, or adverse effects arising from the use or application of the information contained herein. The techniques and suggestions are used at the reader's discretion and are not to be considered a substitute for veterinary care. If you suspect a medical problem consult your veterinarian.

Table of Contents

Chapter 1

Startup Challenges Solved

When you've got your heart set on starting a saltwater aquarium, you don't want any problems to stand between you and the beautiful, thriving system you envision. Still, some setup challenges are inevitable. The good news is that, with a little forethought and planning, you can easily prevent those little bumps in the road from becoming major obstacles to your ultimate success.

Picking the Perfect Place for Your Tank

The best place to put your saltwater tank is wherever it is most aesthetically pleasing to you, right? In actuality, aesthetics are only one piece of the placement puzzle. Other important factors to consider include the amount of weight your floor (or whichever supporting surface you have in mind) can accommodate, the amount of sunlight streaming in from adjacent windows, the presence of heat sources in the room, as well as the amount and types of activities that go on in the immediate vicinity of the tank.

A Weighty Proposition

Depending on the size of the aquarium you intend to set up, the weight exerted on the floor or surface beneath the tank can be quite significant. For our purposes, assume an aquarium weighs about 10 pounds per gallon (about 1.2 kg per liter). That means that a 100-gallon tank weighs about half a ton (100-liter tank weighs about 120 kg), factoring the tank, stand, substrate, decor, and equipment. It's critical to take this weight into consideration to take this weight into consideration when choosing a location for your tank or a stand to place the tank on. For very large systems, it may be necessary to reinforce the floor under the tank so the weight doesn't cause it to sag or buckle.

Don't Let the Sun Shine Down on Your Aquarium

Though some advanced reef aquarists take advantage of natural sunlight to

Always use a manufacturer-recommended stand for your aquarium. It can handle the full weight of a stocked tank.

supplement the lighting for their photosynthetic corals, this is not a good idea for the average fish-only aquarium. In this case, natural sunlight bathing the tank will most likely result in the uncontrollable growth of problem algae. Sunlight can also cause rapid and pronounced water-temperature fluctuations, which are very stressful to tropical marine fishes and other reef organisms. To minimize these potential problems, choose a location for your tank with few or no windows nearby. Also, avoid situating the tank too close to wall vents, registers, or other heat sources that can drive up the water temperature.

What Goes On There?

Place your new saltwater tank in a high-traffic area or the busiest room in the house, and your more shy fish might do a vanishing act, remaining hidden from view as a result of the non-stop activity. The road less traveled usually suits fish better. Moms and dads should advise their kids that boisterous activity or horseplay in the vicinity of the tank can lead to cracked or shattered aquarium glass, which, in turn, can lead to a damaging flood and the untimely death of your specimens—not to mention serious injuries!

Plan For Expansion

A common startup mistake hobbyists make is forgetting to account for future

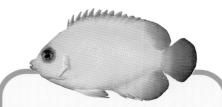

Airborne Pollutants

Don't make the mistake of situating the tank in a location that is subject to airborne contaminants, such as cleaning sprays, cooking oils, hairspray, bug sprays, or other chemical aerosols. Remember, anything that gets in the air will ultimately end up in your aquarium water.

equipment upgrades when setting up a tank. The system you have in place when you start out will, no doubt, evolve over time as you gain experience and begin to experiment with different tools and techniques. During the setup stage, be sure to leave sufficient space behind, around, and beneath your aquarium to accommodate new equipment and any associated cords, hoses, or plumbing.

Thar She Blows!

Aquarium water leaks can range in severity from the subtle dripping of a loose hose connection to the steady trickle of a cracked glass pane or unsealed seam to the powerful gush of a misdirected water pump. However

severe, when leaking salt water and household furnishings or flooring meet, the result can be extensive, costly damage. So how do you make sure the water stays in your tank where it belongs?

Do not stock your tank until you properly test for possible leaks.

Fill 'Er Up

Leaks in brand-new aquariums are very rare occurrences, but they can and do happen as a result of manufacturing defects or careless transportation and handling. After buying your new tank, place it in a location where leaking water can do no harm, such as an outdoor patio, a garage, or an unfinished basement, and fill it completely with fresh water. Monitor the tank for leaks for approximately 24 hours, paying special attention to the corners and seams.

Be sure to dry the exterior of the tank, including the edge trim, with a towel after filling. Water that dribbles from the top and runs down the outside of the tank can collect in the bottom trim and masquerade as a small leak.

Once you're confident that the tank is leak-free, drain the water (you can use it to water plants in your home and garden to avoid waste) and move the tank to the desired setup location in your home.

Keep It on the Level

A tank that is leak-free at setup can still develop a leak over time if it isn't level, because the uneven force of the water pushing on the seams can result in a loss of structural integrity. Before filling the tank, use wooden shims (available at any hardware or home-improvement store) to level the stand as needed. This is a very easy chore to do when the tank is empty but not recommended when it's full.

Carpet presents special challenges when it comes to leveling an aquarium. For one thing, the tack strips used to secure the carpet where the walls and floor meet will tend to pitch the tank forward if you situate it too close to the wall. For another, if the carpet is too thick, the tank may actually rock back and forth whenever anyone walks close by. With taller, more top-heavy tanks, this situation can be extremely dangerous, as the tank can ultimately topple, potentially causing a serious injury or even a fatality.

Check Your Connections

Once your tank is up and running, adopt the habit of looking over all your equipment, hoses, and connections for invisible leaks—perhaps the most common type of aquarium leak. Loose hoses or clamps or poorly sealed PVC pipes are often the culprit here, so check them diligently. Regularly run your hands along the length of each hose or pipe to make sure their exteriors aren't wet to the touch.

We've Got a Geyser!

One way to move water very quickly from your aquarium onto your floor and furnishings is by accidentally bumping or shifting a powerhead or pump return so its flow is briefly directed out of the tank in fountain-like fashion. This is a mistake most hobbyists make only once. After that, they remember to turn off the pumps when doing maintenance work in the tank.

Overcoming Power Struggles

Saltwater aquariums depend on electricity to power heaters, pumps, protein skimmers, filters, lights, and other equipment, so it's vital to ensure during setup that you have easy access to power outlets and a circuit that isn't already overburdened with electrical appliances. Of course, water and electricity are a notoriously deadly combination, so thoughtful steps must be taken to keep them in their separate corners.

Ample Places to Plug In

Make sure you've got outlets in close proximity to your tank so you don't have to run unsightly, and potentially unsafe, extension cords all over your home. Also, keep in mind that you may need to accommodate more equipment down the road should you choose to expand your system. Power strips are a great way to provide additional places to plug in. Just be sure to avoid overtaxing a single circuit by plugging in too many devices.

This Acronym Could Save Your Life!

Your first line of defense against accidental electrical shock is GF(C)I, or Ground Fault (Circuit) Interrupter, technology. Make sure all of your electrical equipment is protected by a GF(C)I, whether at the level of the

Cut Out the Carpet

If you must situate your aquarium in a carpeted room, it might be wise to cut out a section of carpeting to accommodate the "footprint" of the tank. That way, it will be resting on a solid surface, making it much easier to shim and less likely to rock.

What's Sharing the Circuit?

A dedicated circuit is the ideal option for providing power to your aquarium, but this isn't always realistic. However, it's important to consider the amount of power drawn by other appliances and devices sharing the circuit with your aquarium. After all, you don't want to trip the circuit every time someone starts a load of laundry, pops a bag of microwave popcorn, or turns on a hair dryer.

circuit, outlet, or power strip. Here's how one works:

If you look at a typical 120-volt outlet, you'll notice that there's a left slot, a slightly shorter right slot, and a round hole centered beneath the slots. The left slot is considered "neutral," the right slot is "hot," and the hole is ground. When you plug an electrical device or appliance into the outlet, electricity flows from hot to neutral. The job of the GF(C)I is to monitor this flow and to trip the circuit in the event that a mismatch in flow is detected between the hot and neutral.

What does this mean to you, the saltwater aquarium hobbyist? Well, consider what would happen if you were to accidentally drop an energized aquarium light hood into an aquarium full of water. According to human nature, you'd probably reach to grab the fixture, unwittingly forming a direct path for the electricity to flow from the hot wire of the fixture, through your body, and to the ground you're standing on.

Without a GF(C)I, you might be on your way to the great fishroom in the sky, but with one, the change between the hot and neutral slots would be detected instantly, the circuit would be tripped in a tiny fraction of a second, and you'd still be alive to tell the tale.

Get Loopy

Power cords leading from submersible devices, hang-on-tank filters, lighting fixtures and other electrical equipment can serve as a conduit for drips of salt water to flow directly into an outlet or power strip located below the level of the tank, creating the potential for electric shock. A simple solution to this problem is to routinely wipe the cords with a cloth or towel to keep them dry and to tie a loose drip loop in each cord. When a drip loop is in place, water flowing down the cord will accumulate at the lowest part of the loop and drip from there, rather than continue down the cord into the outlet.

Don't Take Chances with Submersible Equipment

Electrical equipment that is actually submerged in water, either partially or completely, presents the greatest risk of causing electrical shock in the event of breakage or malfunction. Submersible glass heaters, for example, can easily be broken by tumbling rocks or a careless hobbyist. Heaters can also drift loose and crack against adjacent rocks if the suction cups that hold them in place become too brittle to maintain suction against the glass. Or, if you forget to unplug a glass heater when doing a water change and it is left exposed to air, it can build up a significant amount of heat. Then, when you bring the water level back to normal, the difference in temperature between the water and heater can cause the glass casing to crack. A rambunctious fish is yet another common cause of heater breakage as well as damage to other submersible equipment.

Whatever the cause, damaged heaters or other submersible equipment can pose a serious shock hazard. To minimize the risk, consider buying a heater made of titanium rather than glass. Also, be aware that some heaters are designed to hang on the rim of the tank and should never be fully submerged. When misbehaving fish are the issue, consider placing your heater out of their reach in a sump below the tank.

If you notice that any submersible device is broken or you suspect it to be faulty, do not put your hands in the water! Unplug the device immediately and replace it with a new one. If you experience a shock when touching the water, stop what you're doing, dry your hands, unplug all electrical equipment, then search for and remove the faulty device.

So Many Ways to Cycle!

For aspiring saltwater aquarists, more confusion arises over the process of cycling than over any other aspect of

Plugging your wires into a GF(C)I is the only option you should consider. If your outlet is not this model, replace it before starting up your aquarium.

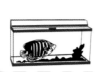

SMALL FRY

Helpful Germs

Parents are always telling kids to wash their hands before they eat and to cover their mouths when they sneeze or cough so they don't spread nasty germs. Cycling an aquarium is a great opportunity to show kids that some germs can actually be helpful!

our hobby. All too often, beginners fail to address this vital step before rushing headlong into stocking fish. After all, the water looks crystal clear, so why wouldn't it be ready for livestock? Unfortunately, the result of skipping this step is predictable—a tank full of dead fish and/or invertebrates. In aquarium hobby parlance, this sudden, seemingly inexplicable loss of specimens is known as "New Tank Syndrome."

Cycling is a process carried out by beneficial aerobic bacteria that makes any aquarium—freshwater or saltwater—suitable for sustaining life. Although it's an invisible process (to the naked eye, anyway), there's really nothing mysterious about it, and it requires more patience than effort on the part of the hobbyist.

Remember the Nitrogen Cycle?

If you remember learning about the nitrogen cycle in school, then this explanation should ring a bell. Cycling begins with the introduction of ammonia to the water. Ammonia, which is extremely toxic to fish and invertebrates, arrives in the form of fish waste or decomposing organic matter of some kind (such as decaying fish food). One type of so-called nitrifying bacteria converts the ammonia to nitrite, which is still toxic to marine life, although less so than ammonia. Then, a second type of nitrifying bacteria converts the nitrite to an even less toxic compound, nitrate. Fish can tolerate low levels of nitrate with no ill effects (corals and other reef invertebrates will respond

adversely to even small amounts of nitrate, however).

Once sufficient colonies of the right kinds of bacteria are present to convert ammonia to nitrite and nitrite to nitrate, your aquarium is cycled. More accurately, you now have a mature biological filter.

Monitoring the Process

But if cycling is an "invisible" process, how will you know that it's proceeding as it should, and, most importantly, when is cycling finished so you can begin stocking (or increasing your stocking level)? Fortunately, you can go to your local aquarium dealer and purchase relatively inexpensive test kits for checking ammonia, nitrite, and nitrate levels in your aquarium water so you'll know with certainty when it's safe to add livestock. With each of these kits, you mix a chemical with a sample of your system water and compare the resultant color of the sample with a color-coded chart included with the kit to determine how much of the compound is present. Here's how it should proceed:

First, you'll measure a spike in the level of ammonia, but nitrite and nitrate will be undetectable. As the first colonies of nitrifying bacteria start to establish themselves (the ones that consume ammonia), the nitrite level will begin to climb as the ammonia level falls. However, you still won't detect nitrate just yet. Next, the ammonia level will drop to zero, and nitrite will spike. As the second form of nitrifying bacteria (which consume nitrite) begins to proliferate, the nitrite level will fall and nitrate will begin to accumulate. Finally, with both forms of bacteria in place and doing their thing, ammonia and nitrite will both be undetectable and nitrate will spike.

Once your tank is cycled you can add your fish. Just remember that the more fish you have in your tank the more ammonia will be produced. Overloading your biofilter will have disastrous consequences.

An Incomplete Cycle?

The astute reader will have noticed that the process described here is not truly a cycle. After all, what happens to the nitrate? That's where you, the hobbyist, come in. You're the final step in the cycle. To prevent nitrate from accumulating to harmful levels, you must perform routine partial water changes—siphoning out some of the polluted water and replacing it with new salt water.

Creating the Right Conditions for Nitrifying Bacteria

As already mentioned, nitrifying bacteria require certain conditions to become established in sufficient numbers in an aquarium. These conditions include surface area to colonize, oxygen-rich water (remember, they're aerobic bacteria), and a source of fuel— the ammonia and nitrite they consume.

Nitrifying bacteria will colonize every surface in the aquarium—glass, substrate, etc.—but to maximize your system's biofiltration capacity, you'll need to provide additional surface area by aquascaping with live rock as well as by utilizing some form of biological filtration medium.

Oxygen-rich water can be provided by creating turbulence at the surface of the aquarium with powerheads or airstones and the return water flow of various filtration devices.

Although it's not their primary function, protein skimmers also do a great job of oxygenating the water. These devices mix air and water in a chamber, causing dissolved pollutants to form a thick foam, which rises to the top of the chamber into a collection cup, where it collapses into yucky brown liquid. The aquarist then empties the cup, thereby removing the dissolved pollutants from the system. Hence, as a result of the protein skimmer's modus operandi, you get water that is both cleaner and well oxygenated.

So-called wet-dry biological filters (also known as trickle filters) are a

Only add fish to your tank once it is fully cycled.

great way to provide both the surface area and oxygen-rich conditions that nitrifying bacteria thrive under. There are many variations on these systems, but they all work in essentially the same way. Water from the aquarium flows down to the biofilter chamber (often located in a sump below the tank) where it collects on a perforated filter plate. From there, it trickles over a porous biological filter medium that provides a large amount of surface area, such as the grooved plastic spheres known in the hobby as bio balls. The dry part of the wet-dry designation is a bit misleading, however. While it's true that the biofilter medium is never fully submerged, it is kept continuously moist by the water trickling over it.

Sources of Ammonia

The third requirement of nitrifying bacteria—a source of ammonia to get the whole cycle started—can be provided in a number of ways. For instance, you can feed the tank some fresh, frozen, or flake food just as you would if fish were already present. The decomposition of the food should produce enough ammonia to kick-start the cycle. Another option is to add ammonia directly by dosing the tank with ammonium chloride (available at any chemical supply store).

A long-standing method of cycling a marine aquarium involves the

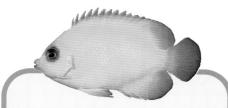

Borrow Some Bacteria

An easy, time-tested way to introduce colonies of nitrifying bacteria and get your biofilter on the road to maturity is to add a few handfuls of substrate or some filter media from an established aquarium that already has a mature biofilter.

introduction of a few extremely hardy fishes—typically damsels—to the system so that the ammonia in their waste products will get the bio ball rolling, so to speak. But this approach is problematic for two reasons. One, subjecting damsels to high levels of ammonia and nitrite hardly seems humane—even if they can survive such treatment. Two, most damsels are highly territorial and will savagely defend their territory, which may include the whole tank, against all comers, regardless of size. This behavior can be a problem when you're ready to introduce more specimens. Usually, it's necessary to remove the damsel and either return it to the dealer or attempt to reintroduce it after the new fishes have had a chance to get established.

A Rock-Solid Approach to Cycling

A much more humane method of introducing ammonia is using live rocks. Live rocks are porous chunks of reef rubble that have broken away from the main reef structure as a result of storms, surging waves, and other natural processes. These rocks are commonly used to form the basic rockwork foundation in saltwater aquariums.

The term *live* refers not to the rocks themselves but to the myriad encrusting organisms residing on and within high-quality specimens. These might include various forms of micro- and macroalgae, polyps, sponges, worms, snails, crustaceans, tunicates, bryozoans, sea stars and brittle stars, and a host of other encrusting creatures. Because of their porous nature, live rocks also tend to be heavily colonized with nitrifying bacteria—the key players in the cycling process.

Using damsels to cycle your tank is a cruel practice. Opt instead for fishless cycling.

So how do live rocks help with the introduction of ammonia to the system? Well, when you remove live rocks from nature, expose them to air, subject them to the rigors of shipping (typically wrapped in wet newspaper and stuffed in boxes), and then acclimate them to completely different conditions in the aquarium, some die-off of those encrusting organisms is unavoidable. You can take advantage of that die-off, and the ammonia it produces, to initiate the cycling process, which will be helped along by the bacterial colonies already present on the live rocks.

What Should I Do With This Box of Rocks?

When that box of live rocks arrives on your doorstep, or you bring some home from your local fish store, you might think to yourself, "Now what?" Well, before they can be used in a stocked system, live rocks must be cured. That is, the die-off previously described must be allowed to take place under controlled conditions—such as in a separate plastic bin or in a new aquarium that is being cycled. Uncured rocks should never be placed in a stocked aquarium, or you risk losing your valued specimens to ammonia poisoning.

Clean 'Em Up!

When cleaning live rocks, your goal should be to keep as many organisms alive as possible while removing any dead or dying organisms that you can spot. When your rocks arrive, unpack them promptly, and spread them out on a plastic tarp—preferably outdoors because this can get messy. Have on hand clean scrub brushes of various sizes (a toothbrush is ideal for hard-to-reach spaces), a plastic bucket filled about three-quarters full with salt water, a plastic spray bottle filled with salt water, and a large plastic bin filled about half way with salt water. The bin will function as your curing vat and should be situated in a protected location in your home where it can remain for several weeks.

Using your brushes, scrub away any obviously dead and decomposing organisms, which will likely appear as a slimy white film. In between scrubbings, dip the rock in the bucket of salt water to rinse off loosened debris. Then, place the cleaned rock into the plastic bin and move on to the next piece of rock. To keep the rocks from drying out on the tarp, mist them regularly with salt water using your plastic spray bottle.

As you're cleaning, scan among the rocks for any live-rock stowaways that you don't want in your tank, such as mantis shrimp, stone crabs, fireworms, and other nasties, that might have dropped onto the tarp (more on these in Chapter 5). Exercise due caution when removing any suspicious critters (wear gloves, use tongs or tweezers, etc.) as some are capable of stinging or wounding the careless handler.

Into the Curing Bin

After all of your rocks have been scrubbed clean of decomposing gunk and placed in the plastic bin, top off the bin with salt water so that all of the rocks are completely submerged. Then, place a powerhead in the bin to circulate water

Pre-Cured or Uncured?

Live rock is sold as either pre-cured or uncured. With pre-cured rocks, the live rock operator oversees the initial die-off process, while with uncured rocks, this chore is left to the consumer (which is why they're much less expensive). Be aware, however, that a small amount of die-off will occur with pre-cured rocks, so some additional curing will still be required on your part.

Live rock is usually shipped wrapped in wet newspaper.

through the live rocks. Just as with cycling, the ongoing decomposition that takes place during the curing process will result in consecutive spikes of ammonia, nitrite, and nitrate, and you'll need to monitor this progression with your test kits so that you can tell when the process is complete—that is, once ammonia and nitrite are no longer detectable.

During the curing process, it's a good idea to perform water changes about twice a week in order to siphon out any debris that has settled to the bottom of the bin and to keep the ammonia level from spiking so high that it kills the desirable encrusting organisms that you're trying to preserve.

Depending on a number of factors, such as whether the rocks are purchased uncured or pre-cured and how good a job you do of cleaning off decaying organic matter, you can expect curing to take anywhere from two to six weeks to run its course.

Stacking and Stabilizing the Rockwork

As mentioned earlier, live rocks are commonly used as the basic foundation of a saltwater aquarium, especially in reef systems and so-called FOWLR (Fish Only With Live Rock) systems. FOWLR tanks are really catching on in the hobby because they are much more naturalistic than the old-fashioned tank full of bleached coral skeletons could ever be.

As a cost-cutting measure, you can also opt to use non-live rocks, or so-called base rocks, to start your rockwork foundation and then place the more costly live rocks on top of them.

Whichever approach you choose, it's important to arrange your rocks in a manner that is visually pleasing to you, provides ample retreats and hiding places for the fish, and allows water circulation to reach all areas of the tank.

Don't Forget Displacement!

Just as plopping ice cubes into a beverage causes the fluid level in your glass to rise, the rocks you place in your tank will displace a volume of water equal to their own volume. Simply put, don't fill your tank completely with salt water and then try to add the rocks or your floor will be

Live rock can form the basis of your biofiltration.

inundated. A better option is to fill the tank only half way before adding the rocks. You can always top off the tank with more water as needed once the rocks are in place. Better yet, put your rocks in place with the tank completely empty. This approach makes it much easier to firmly stabilize the rocks to one another before water is added. But don't forget to mist the rocks frequently with salt water while you're arranging them so that they don't dry out.

Go For the Honeycomb Effect

If our aquascaping objective is to have lots of nooks, crannies, caves, and hidey holes while allowing good water circulation, building the standard wall of rock would not be ideal. Instead, try to create a more open framework, resembling a honeycomb rather than a solid wall.

Also, don't forget that fish need room to swim. If possible, leave room behind, alongside, and in front of the rockwork so the fish can swim in an uninterrupted circular pattern instead of having to turn around at either end of the tank. Alternatively, you can provide a figure-eight swimming pattern by building two separate rock stacks with open space in between.

Building on the Shifting Sands

If you plan to include a substrate, such as sand or crushed coral, in your aquarium, you'll need to decide whether you want to add the substrate first and then place the rocks on top of the substrate or build the rock pile first and then spread the substrate around the rocks. There are special considerations for both approaches.

If you add the substrate first, the rock pile above will tend to be less stable and can be undermined by digging, burrowing, and sand-sifting fishes and/or invertebrates. To help minimize the likelihood of an avalanche resulting from the shifting sands, your rockwork can be stabilized by placing short sections of PVC pipe in strategic locations in the substrate.

On the other hand, if you place the rocks directly on the glass tank bottom, you run a greater risk of chipping or cracking the glass should a rock take a tumble. In this case, securing the bottom layer of rocks to the glass with a few dabs of aquarium-safe silicone will help keep the pile in place. A sort of middle of the road between these two approaches is to put a thinner layer of substrate material beneath the rocks to act as a shock absorber and then apply a thicker layer around the rest of the tank bottom.

Wrap It Up

Not only should the rocks in your aquascaping be stable relative to the substrate, but they should also be stable relative to each other—especially if you plan to keep any large, cantankerous fish species that might be inclined to ransack their surroundings. Silicone and plastic cable ties are both very useful tools for this purpose. And don't be too concerned that the ties will be visible and disrupt the naturalistic look of your tank. In time, they'll become completely camouflaged by an attractive patina of pink coralline algae.

Chapter 2

Stocking Challenges Solved

Many of the challenges associated with stocking a saltwater aquarium stem from failing to do your homework before buying specimens. The temptation to buy beautiful or exotic-looking fish or invertebrates on impulse and without prior knowledge of their care requirements, habits, and temperament can be very difficult to resist, even for the experienced aquarist.

Serious disease issues can crop up when we fail to recognize tell-tale symptoms or when we fail to quarantine specimens properly. But you don't have to make these costly, common errors. This chapter will get you thinking about some of the important considerations of livestock selection and acclimation.

Characteristics of a Healthy Fish

Knowing what healthy fish are supposed to look like is a key to selecting specimens that will thrive in your aquarium. Don't make the mistake of looking at a sickly fish and convincing yourself that, with just a little TLC, you'll be able to bring it back around. In all probability, you won't succeed. The most likely outcome is that the ailing fish will ultimately succumb to the stress of being acclimated to yet another set of conditions in your aquarium. So, what should you look for when shopping for fish?

The following questions should be asked before settling for any specimen.

Is the Fish Behaving Normally?

Behaving normally can mean different things for different fish species. For example, it would be normal for the shy comet, or marine betta, *Calloplesiops altivelis,* to hide behind rocks or other tank decor as opposed to swimming in full view at the front of the tank. On the other hand, bolder species, such as the various damsels or hawkfishes, should be more active and visible (assuming they've been given a little time to acclimate). In general, though, look for lively, energetic specimens that appear reactive to

Calloplesiops altivelis *is a shy fish, so don't be surprised if you rarely see it out and about.*

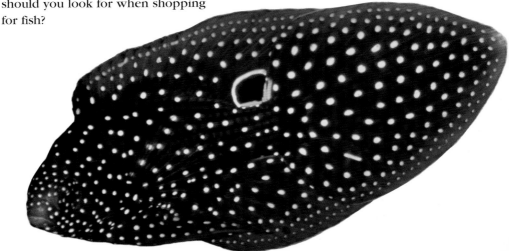

what's going on around them—such as you approaching the tank. Specimens that appear listless or seem to be swimming erratically should be avoided.

Do You See Any Symptoms of Disease or Parasites?

Not all fish diseases or parasites will be readily apparent from a visual inspection at your local fish store. Still, there are certain red flags you can look for. Does the fish's respiration seem to be unusually high? Is the fish shimmying, dashing about the tank, or repeatedly scraping its body on objects in the tank? Do you see any tiny white spots, velvety patches, or ulcerations on the fish's body? Are its eyes clouded or bulging? Are its fins tattered, torn, notched, or otherwise incomplete? Do you observe any lumps or growths that aren't typical of the species? If you answer "yes" to any of these questions—or if you observe any other worrying symptoms—don't buy the fish.

Do Other Fish in the Tank Exhibit Symptoms?

In some cases, the fish you've got your eye on may look perfectly healthy, but other specimens in the tank are either deceased or exhibiting one or more of the disease symptoms just described. If you see dead fish or any signs of illness in the display tank, you can safely assume that all the fish in the tank are

Choosing Fish by the Book

Take a good marine fish ID book with you when you shop (or ask if your dealer has one handy) so you can see what the fish are supposed to look like when they are healthy.

infected and that the one you're interested in just hasn't begun to show symptoms yet. When it comes to choosing healthy specimens, always err on the side of caution.

Is the Fish Eating?

Getting fish to feed can be problematic at times, and it's not unheard of for a specimen to refuse all foods offered to the point of starvation and death. To sidestep this discouraging scenario, ask your dealer to feed the fish while you're there so that you can verify that it is, indeed, eating. Most reputable dealers will be happy to accommodate you in this regard (if not, take your business elsewhere). If the fish was already fed that day, offer to put some earnest money down to hold the fish and come back another day at the scheduled feeding time.

Is It Starved Beyond Salvation?

A fish that has a severely pinched-in belly has likely been starved to the point that it will not survive despite your best efforts, even if it

A mandarinfish needs a well established 200-gallon (800-liter) or larger aquaium with plenty of live rock and no direct competitors in order to find enough food to survive—they almost never make it.

demonstrates a willingness to feed. This problem is especially common among species that need to forage continuously throughout the day, such as the mandarinfish, *Synchiropus splendidus*. When choosing a fish of any species, always look for a robust-bodied specimen with a filled-out or rounded belly, which suggests it hasn't missed too many meals.

Should You Buy Captive-Raised Specimens?

Although the collection of marine fishes for the aquarium trade has a very modest impact on the health of coral reefs (provided it is done in a legal manner using sustainable methods), these fragile ecosystems are in genuine crisis around the globe, so anything we

can do to minimize collection pressure is both good for the reefs and good for our hobby. Toward that end, we should try to purchase captive-raised specimens instead of wild-caught ones whenever possible.

Various clownfishes, basslets, cardinalfishes, blennies, gobies, dottybacks, seahorses, and other species are currently being raised by commercial breeders. Although the list of captive-raised species may not be extensive right now, it is growing and will continue to grow as long as we support the aquaculture industry with our dollars. Captive-raised specimens may cost a bit more, but in the long run the benefits more than justify the added expense.

In addition to relieving collection

pressure on the world's coral reefs, captive-raised specimens are already acclimated to aquarium conditions, readily accept standard aquarium fare, and have a better survival record, which means you don't have to continually shell out money to replace dead specimens.

The Quarantine Tank

After making the investment in a saltwater aquarium, the budding hobbyist may question the necessity of setting up a second tank for the purpose of quarantining new specimens. But that initial investment is precisely what makes a quarantine tank so important. By spending a very modest amount for a basic quarantine system now, you might save yourself hundreds, if not thousands, of dollars down the road by preventing the introduction of pathogens or parasites that might infect and kill all of your aquarium livestock.

Why We Quarantine

A quarantine tank serves two important purposes. One, it allows you to keep specimens in isolation for several weeks so that you can observe them for signs of disease or parasites that weren't evident at the time of purchase. Two, if the fish does prove to be infected, the quarantine tank can

In the wild a clownfish cannot survive without its host anemone, but it will thrive in an aquarium without one, which is fortunate because as easy as it is to keep a clownfish, an anemone rarely survives in captivity.

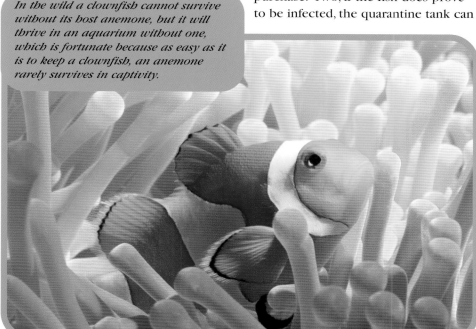

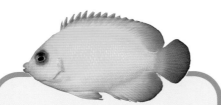

because they kill bacteria, they can have an adverse impact on your biological filter.

Keep It Simple

In many cases, a standard 10-gallon (40-liter) tank will suffice for a quarantine system, but you may need to go as large as 40 gallons (160 liters), depending on the size of the fish you're quarantining. No substrate is necessary, or desirable, in the tank, but be sure to provide some hiding places in the form of PVC pipe sections or new (never used before) flower pots turned on their sides.

Other necessities include a heater, filter (a basic sponge or hang-on-tank filter will suffice), and some means for providing water movement and aeration, such as an airstone and air pump or a powerhead positioned near the top of the tank. Lighting is optional—and can be unsettling to skittish specimens that have just been introduced to quarantine—but will make it easier to visually examine fish for signs of disease or parasites. To provide biological filtration in the quarantine tank, you can borrow bacteria-inoculated media from your display tank filtration system. One popular approach is to keep some extra filter media in the display aquarium's sump as standard practice so that whenever you need it you can just grab this ready-made biofilter. Also, be sure to perform copious water changes during the quarantine process, taking care to siphon out any fish feces or uneaten

The Consequences of Skipping Quarantine

If you fail to quarantine and, instead, immediately introduce a fish to your display tank, any ailment that crops up will infect all of your fish, not just a single specimen. And, with some parasites and pathogens, the result can be the loss of all your valued livestock.

be converted immediately to a hospital tank so you can more easily treat and cure it before introducing it to the main aquarium.

Should You Medicate Your Main System?

Medicating your main system is not a desirable alternative. Fish vary in their sensitivity to medications, and some common treatments can do more harm than good when used indiscriminately. For example, copper, which is very effective in treating parasites, can be harmful to some fish species that lack scales, such as various blennies, gobies, dragonets, and puffers, and downright deadly to invertebrates. Antibiotics can also be harmful to invertebrates, and food, to prevent dissolved pollutant levels from overwhelming the biofilter and further stressing (or killing) your new fish.

Match Water Conditions

Since your quarantined specimen is destined to be moved within a matter of weeks to your display tank, you'll want to make sure the water parameters in your quarantine tank—temperature, specific gravity, pH, etc.—mirror those of the display tank. The best and easiest way to achieve this is to fill the quarantine tank with water siphoned directly from your display tank.

How Long Should You Quarantine?

As with so many aspects of the saltwater aquarium hobby, opinions on the appropriate duration for quarantine vary from one expert to the next. Any period of quarantine is better than none, but four weeks should be sufficient time for any problems to become apparent and will serve as a good benchmark.

You've Bought a Fish on Impulse. Now What?

Okay, even though you know you should thoroughly research every livestock purchase to make sure you

A quarantine tank does not have to be large nor does it need to be intricately decorated.

Always research the fish you want to keep before actually buying them. By doing so you will learn all you need to know about caring for your fish. Only research could tell you that the bluehead wrasse, Thalassoma bifasciatum, *can be territorial and should be introduced after more peaceful species.*

can provide for the specimen's needs and so you won't create any compatibility issues in your aquarium, you've gone ahead and bought a fish without first doing your homework. Now the excitement of your new acquisition is giving way to buyer's remorse because it's occurring to you that you don't have the slightest clue what (or if) this fish will eat or how it will behave in captivity. What should you do now?

Research: Better Late Than Never

Hit the books anyway! Hopefully, you've isolated the specimen in a quarantine tank, so you have at least a small window of opportunity to learn about the species from various books, magazines, online resources, your dealer (who, frankly, should have told

you what to expect from the species in first place), or other hobbyists before it's time to introduce it to your display tank.

If you're lucky, you might just discover that the fish will accept most standard aquarium foods and will get along fine with the other fish in your system, in which case you can proceed through quarantine and then introduce the fish to your tank at the appropriate time. On the other hand, you may find out that you really can't accommodate the species' dietary needs or that it will be either too aggressive or too passive to coexist with your other fish. In this case, your best option is to return the fish to your dealer and ask for a refund or store credit. Even if your dealer won't agree to a refund or credit, you're better off losing what you paid for a single fish than having to replace all of your livestock following tank-wide compatibility and aggression issues.

If, instead of quarantining, you immediately introduced the bought-on-impulse specimen to your main tank only to discover too late that you've made an unwise purchase, you should still remove the specimen. But now you've got another potential problem on your hands (besides the added difficulty of capturing a fish that has a live rock labyrinth to hide in): the fish may have introduced a disease or parasite to the main system during its short stay. That means you'll need to keep a very sharp eye on all your fish for the next several weeks to make sure they don't begin to show symptoms of infection—and be prepared to remove any ailing specimens to a hospital tank for treatment.

Avoiding "Shoehorn Tank Syndrome"

Just as you must resist the temptation to buy specimens without first researching their needs, you must also resist the admittedly compelling urge to keep adding just one more fish to an already fully stocked aquarium. To do so will overwhelm your biofilter so that it cannot keep pace with the dissolved pollutants produced by the fishes, and you'll end up causing a deadly ammonia spike. Also, oxygen depletion occurs very rapidly in an

overstocked tank because the fish will use up the dissolved oxygen faster than it can be replenished from the atmosphere. Furthermore, the more fish you shoehorn into a confined space, the more compatibility issues that are likely to arise as territories begin to overlap. So, how do you know when to say when when it comes to stocking?

The Old Inch-of-Fish-Per-Gallon-of-Water Rule

Unfortunately, there's no simple formula you can use to determine reliably how many fish you can keep in a given volume of water. You may have heard the old rule of not exceeding one inch of fish per gallon

SMALL FRY

A Long, Long Life

Many saltwater fish can live a surprisingly long time in the aquarium. Reports of specimens living for 10 to 15 years (or even longer!) are not uncommon. That means if you buy a fish when your child is in preschool and give it the best possible care, it might still be around when your child heads off to college!

Despite its extreme appeal, the clown triggerfish, Balistoides conspicillum, *is unlikely to work out in your aquarium. That fetching juvenile will soon be a bloodthirsty, 20-inch (50-cm) monster.*

of water or some variation thereupon (and there are many variations), but any such guideline is, quite frankly, useless. Why? Because total body length reveals very little about the impact a fish will have on water quality.

For example, five 3-inch (7.5-cm) blue-green chromis, *Chromis viridis*, and one 15-inch (38-cm) spotted scat, *Scatophagus argus,* would be equal in total body length, but that single trigger would, without a doubt, be a much bigger polluter than the five chromis combined. Hence, you must consider the overall mass of a specimen and its dietary habits to get a sense of how much dissolved waste it will contribute to the system.

Room to Swim and a Place to Stake a Claim

The availability of swimming space and territorial niches will impact the number and types of fish your system can accommodate, as well. On the one hand, if much of your tank's available space is taken up by live rock, you

rockwork, fish that need to have a hiding place close at hand may be hard pressed to find the cover they need.

Use the Introduce-and-Observe Method

While standby formulas are of little use in determining proper stocking rates for the saltwater aquarium, there is a method you can use to avoid Shoehorn Tank Syndrome, and all it takes is patience and some careful observation on your part.

Specimens should be introduced gradually, one species at a time. Allow a few weeks to pass in between introductions (this is the part that takes patience), and be sure to test your water diligently to make sure the ammonia level doesn't spike after each specimen is introduced.

You should observe that each fish stakes out a particular region in the tank—perhaps a cave in the live rock, a burrow in the substrate, or a particular area of open water. Pay close attention to where these territorial boundaries end or overlap. Once it becomes

won't be able to keep many fish needing ample swimming room, such as the various surgeonfishes. On the other hand, if you have an abundance of swimming space but minimal

Why Not Just Float the Bag?

You may have learned that floating a bagged fish in your aquarium water for a half hour or so is a good way to acclimate the specimen. But this approach could be described as partial acclimation at best because it only serves to equalize the water temperature between the bag and the aquarium. It doesn't address all the other important water parameters, such as salinity and pH.

apparent that the territorial opportunities have all been taken up and it's evident through testing that the biological filter is keeping pace with the stocking level, or bioload, stop adding new specimens—and don't be surprised if it takes fewer fish than you might expect to reach this point.

Drip Your Way to Successful Acclimation

The coral reefs are among the most stable environments on earth. By logical extension, fish and invertebrates collected from the reefs are intolerant of rapidly fluctuating water conditions. Because it's likely that the water in your dealer's tanks differs markedly from the water in your tank, it's vital to acclimate new specimens slowly and gradually to your water conditions before releasing them into your tank (either display or quarantine). That's best accomplished through drip acclimation.

The Drip-Acclimation Process

To get set up for drip acclimation, you'll need the following materials:
- rigid plastic container that can accommodate your specimen and at least double the volume of water in the specimen bag
- flexible airline tubing
- plastic airline control valve

Gently pour the water and fish from the plastic bag into the rigid plastic container. The container should be narrow enough across the bottom so the fish remains completely submerged in water. Place the container below the level of the aquarium. Connect two lengths of airline tubing with the airline control valve. If you don't have a control valve, you can simply tie a few loose knots in the middle of one long section of tubing. Next, place one end of the tubing in the aquarium and extend the other end down to the plastic container.

You do not need to suck on the free end of the airline tubing to start the siphon! Why risk a mouthful of yucky aquarium water? Instead, simply place the opening of the top end into the discharge of a powerhead or other water pump. In seconds, the

water will begin flowing, and you can quickly restrict the flow to a few drips per second by adjusting the airline valve or tightening the knots.

Continue dripping aquarium water into the container that holds your specimen until you double the volume of water that came in the bag. Then, drain out half of the water and resume dripping until the water volume doubles again. Next, test the salinity, temperature, and pH of the water in the container and compare the values to those in your display aquarium. If they still differ, repeat the dripping and testing process until they come into balance. Once they match, you're finished acclimating, and you can net out the fish and release it into your tank. Avoid dumping the dirty water from your acclimation container into the main tank or you'll introduce any pollutants, pathogens, or parasites that might have come from your dealer's tank into your healthy system.

Expect the Unexpected!

Even when you do all the necessary research and follow all the rules for proper stocking and quarantine, it's still possible for unanticipated problems to develop. As they say in the zoo biz, animals don't read books. They don't know (or care) how they're supposed to behave in the aquarium setting. And, as they say in the advertising biz, results may vary. Each specimen of a given species is an individual, and while one may prove to be a model aquarium citizen, another may cause more than its share of headaches. So don't be surprised if the occasional specimen defies conventional wisdom by behaving worse (or better) than you might expect.

Chapter 3

Water Quality and Chemistry
Conundrums Solved

Water is to aquarium life as air is to humans and other land dwellers. Just as our survival is dependent upon the chemical makeup and quality of the air we breathe, saltwater organisms must have water of the correct chemistry and quality if they are to survive and remain in good health. And since the majority of the saltwater fish and invertebrates we keep in our aquariums come from one of the most stable environments on earth—the tropical coral reef—we can reason logically that their water chemistry and quality must be kept clean and stable within acceptable ranges, as well.

The Trouble with Tap Water

Sometimes the source of a water-quality problem is, well, the source itself—the water from the tap, that is. While water straight from the tap is perfectly safe for people to drink, it cannot be used for sustaining delicate marine life. Before it's safe to use in the aquarium, tap water must first be treated to remove or neutralize potentially harmful chemicals and contaminants.

Is Dechlorinating the Water Sufficient?

For the fish-only system, the very least you must do is treat your tap water with a dechlorinating product to remove or neutralize the chlorine and/or chloramine that are added to municipal water supplies to prevent the growth of harmful bacteria. Make sure the product you choose is formulated to remove both chemicals!

However, while dechlorinating alone may make your tap water safe for fish, it leaves behind many other potential contaminants, such as nitrate, phosphate, silicate, iron, copper, lead, and other impurities, which can either contribute to outbreaks of problem algae or kill invertebrates outright. Frankly, we can do better for our saltwater fish.

Treating your water removes harmful chemicals and elements.

RO/DI Systems

The best way to eliminate the great unknown when it comes to your tap water is to process it through a reverse osmosis (RO) unit, a deionizing (DI) unit, or, better yet, a system that combines both (RO/DI).

With RO units, your tap water is forced under pressure through a semipermeable membrane, which traps impurities and contaminants. Because this process involves the movement of water from an area with a higher concentration of dissolved solids across a membrane to an area with a lower concentration of dissolved solids, it is called reverse osmosis. In regular osmosis, the opposite occurs—water moves from an area with a lower concentration of dissolved solids to an area with a higher concentration of dissolved solids.

DI units pass the tap water through a deionizing resin, which forms a chemical bond with contaminants (a process known as adsorption), thereby removing them from the water. Many companies combine both RO and DI units in a single system. These systems often include a sediment filter and carbon filter to prefilter the water before it reaches the RO and DI units, prolonging the life of the RO membrane and DI resin.

The RO/DI-purified water can then be used to mix salt water for filling a new tank or performing a water change. It should also be used

> ### Reclaiming RO/DI Waste Water
>
> RO/DI units produce a lot of "waste water." That is, most of the water flowing from your tap will be discharged through a wastewater line. Rather than allow this waste to run down the drain, you can collect it in a bucket and use it for other purposes, such as watering your garden or for household cleaning chores.

whenever you top off your tank with fresh water to replace the water lost to evaporation.

How Do You Know What's in Your Water?

Staying abreast of water quality or chemical fluctuations requires regular monitoring of water parameters with quality test kits. At the very minimum, you'll need test kits for ammonia, nitrite, nitrate, pH, calcium, and alkalinity.

Do not settle for the cheapest kits money can buy! The accuracy and reliability of test kits can vary considerably from one brand to the next. The experiences of your dealer and fellow hobbyists can be a good guide in helping you choose kits with a solid reputation for producing accurate, reliable results.

Also, be aware that test kits that use chemical reagents have a limited shelf life. If you use them beyond the expiration date, you may get inaccurate results, and you might end up missing a problem or making changes to correct a problem that doesn't necessarily exist.

Comparing Colors

Most test protocols involve the addition of one or more chemical reagents to a sample of aquarium water and then observing the sample for a color change. With so-called color-comparison kits, you simply add a specified amount of reagent to the sample and then compare the resultant color to a chart or chip that is included with the kit. With titration kits, you add the reagent drop by drop until the sample takes on a particular color. The reading is determined by the number of drops it takes to reach that color.

The drawback to both color-comparison and titration test kits is that the results are, to at least some degree, in the eye of the beholder. Some hobbyists find it difficult to make an exact match between the color of the sample and the subtle color gradations on the chart or chip. The color often appears to fall somewhere in between.

Going Digital

A more accurate method of testing certain water parameters is to use electronic monitors that take readings via a probe placed in the aquarium water. These units provide a digital readout, eliminating the guesswork associated with kits that depend upon color comparison. With the better digital units, you get much greater accuracy, provided you calibrate and clean them properly, but there is a tradeoff in cost as they are significantly more expensive than colorimetric test kits.

Help! My Specific Gravity is Unstable!

Since this book is a saltwater problem solver, the first water-chemistry

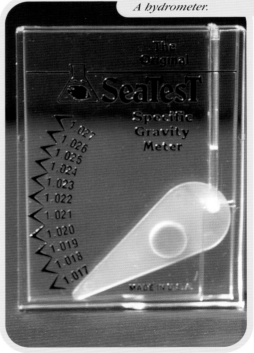

A hydrometer.

conundrum we'll tackle is unstable salinity. Actually, what we'll be looking at is specific gravity, an indirect measurement of salinity, which is very easy to test using an instrument called a hydrometer.

A hydrometer reads the density of water, comparing the weight of a sample of salt water to the weight of an equal volume of distilled water. The easiest style of hydrometer to use is the swing-needle hydrometer. With swing-needle units, all you have to do is fill the hydrometer to a predetermined level with saltwater and observe where the needle eventually settles. The higher it rises, the higher the specific gravity of the sample.

The desired specific gravity range for a fish-only tank is 1.022 to 1.025. It's best to choose one target reading within the range and strive to maintain that level without fluctuations. However, several factors can conspire to raise or lower your specific gravity from that target reading.

Evaporation

When water evaporates from a saltwater aquarium, all of the salt dissolved in the water gets left behind. Only the pure, fresh water evaporates. The more evaporation that occurs, the higher the specific gravity in the aquarium will rise. To compensate for evaporation, top off your aquarium with purified fresh water every day. Make sure the volume

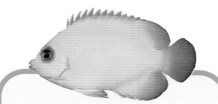

Make Your Mark

An easy trick that will help ensure that you don't miss the mark when you top off with fresh water is to literally make a mark (or place a piece of tape) on your aquarium or sump at the desired full level. Whenever evaporation lowers your water level—and it will every day— simply add fresh water until the level is even with the mark.

of the top-off water exactly matches the volume of water lost to evaporation or you'll either lower the specific gravity below the target valve by adding too much or fail to reach the target by adding too little.

Salt Creep

A small amount of salt will be removed from the system through a process known as salt creep, thus lowering your specific gravity over time. Salt creep is a crusty buildup of salt that develops on any aquarium or equipment surface that is exposed to both air and saltwater spray—such as that caused by filter returns, powerheads, or bubbling airstones. Creep is a good description, as this is a slow process that lowers specific gravity very gradually.

To counteract the specific-gravity-lowering effect of salt creep, you may need to add a small amount of aquarium salt to your system occasionally. Simply dissolve the salt in your purified top-off water and drip it slowly into your tank or sump. Alternatively, over the course of several water changes, you can mix your replacement water to a slightly higher-than-normal specific gravity to bring the specific gravity of your aquarium back to the desired level gradually.

Saltwater Mixing Mishaps

A very common cause of fluctuating specific gravity is replacing aquarium water removed during a partial water change with salt water of a lower or higher specific gravity. In some instances, this is due to carelessness or "close enough" thinking on the part of the aquarist, but more often than not, it's a result of impatience.

If you mix a batch of salt water and immediately take a hydrometer reading, it's unlikely that you'll get an accurate specific-gravity measurement. You must give the salt time to dissolve completely before you can expect to get an accurate

hydrometer reading. This is best accomplished by waiting for approximately 24 hours while circulating and aerating the water with a powerhead or airstone. Then, test again and add either more salt or more fresh water if necessary before doing your water change.

My pH Won't Stay Put!

The pH of your aquarium water is another important parameter you'll

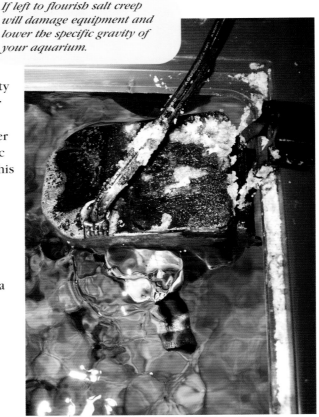

If left to flourish salt creep will damage equipment and lower the specific gravity of your aquarium.

need to monitor and work to keep stable. In any discussion of aquarium pH, you'll also hear mention of the term *alkalinity*, as the two parameters are interrelated.

In simple terms, pH is a measure of how acidic or basic your water is. Measured on a scale from zero to 14, a pH value of 7.0 is considered neutral while values below 7.0 are acidic and values above 7.0 are basic. The preferred pH range for a saltwater aquarium is 8.2 to 8.4.

Aquarium Antacids

Alkalinity, or buffering capacity, can be defined as your water's ability to resist a change in pH and is determined by the amount of buffering compounds (primarily carbonates) present in the water. The recommended alkalinity range is between 7 and 10 dKH.

Think of buffering agents as antacids for your aquarium. The more acids that are introduced to the water, the more these buffers are depleted. In the saltwater aquarium, it's this depletion of buffers that tends to drive pH down from the desirable range.

Going Overboard on the Bioload

An overstocked, overfed tank is much more prone to plummeting pH than is a tank with an appropriate bioload because of the excessive acids introduced through waste material, metabolic processes of the livestock, and rotting, uneaten food. The solution here? Stock and feed lightly!

Insufficient Aeration

Carbon dioxide, which is acidic and drives down pH, can accumulate in aquariums that lack sufficient aeration and water circulation. This can be especially problematic in taller tanks, which tend to have a poor water-volume-to-surface-area ratio and, therefore, don't allow adequate gas exchange at the surface.

To maximize aeration:
- Choose a long, horizontal tank with greater surface area.
- Take advantage of filter return hoses and/or powerheads to create turbulence at the water surface.
- Use submerged powerheads to circulate oxygenated water throughout the entire tank.
- Include a protein skimmer and wet-

dry biofilter—both of which do a great job of aerating the water—in your water-purification arsenal.

Overdue Water Change

Even in an appropriately stocked aquarium, the pH will gradually trend downward if you don't stay on top of those routine partial water changes, which not only help to replenish depleted buffering compounds (they're included in the sea-salt mix), but also remove fish waste and uneaten food before they decompose and foul the water. In addition to stocking and feeding lightly, routine partial water changes are your best defense against pH fluctuations. Be sure to change at least 20 percent of your aquarium's water volume every month.

Holy Spiking Ammonia!

Wait a minute! Didn't we leave spiking ammonia behind back in Chapter 1? After all, the cycling process has long been completed. Aren't those nitrifying bacteria still doing their job, converting ammonia to nitrite and nitrite to

nitrate? Why do we need to worry about ammonia anymore? Remember, biofiltration can easily be thrown out of balance if the level of dissolved pollutants that fuel the process suddenly increases to the extent that the nitrifying bacteria can no longer keep pace. When this happens, the resultant ammonia spike can cause the death of valued specimens. So, don't put away your ammonia test kit just yet!

Addition of a Specimen

Giving in to the temptation to add just one more fish can easily lead to an ammonia spike if your biological filter is already straining to keep pace with a large population of livestock— especially if you add more than one specimen or a single larger specimen with a hefty appetite to match. The number of specimens you introduce must not exceed your aquarium's carrying capacity, which is determined both by the availability of territorial space within the system as well as the ability of your biofilter

Nighttime pH Drop is Normal

If you test your aquarium's pH at night just before lights out and again in the morning just before turning the lights back on, you may notice that the pH has dropped slightly. This occurs because, at night, the algae in your tank take in oxygen and produce carbon dioxide but do not consume carbon dioxide and produce oxygen from photosynthesis as they do in the daytime. This drives down pH.

to keep pace with the pollutants produced by the livestock.

Death of a Specimen

One of the most common causes of spiking ammonia is the presence of a dead, decomposing fish or other organism in the system. Any deceased specimen should be removed promptly upon discovery. Often, though, a sick fish will conceal itself somewhere in the rockwork and perish there. If the hobbyist is not attentive, the rotting fish will cause an ammonia spike before its death is even discovered. Be sure to take a head count of your fish every day and, if a specimen turns up missing, promptly launch the recovery mission.

Feeding Foibles

Our fish can easily dupe us into overfeeding by behaving as if they're on the verge of starvation every time we approach the tank. Don't give in to this shameless display! Not only is overfeeding directly harmful to your fish's health, but it's also indirectly harmful because any uneaten food will decompose and foul the water, leading to an ammonia spike.

Adding Uncured Live Rock

If you decide to spruce up your aquascaping by adding a few new pieces of live rock, make sure they are fully cured before placing them in your tank. Remember, some additional die-off of the organisms encrusting live rock is inevitable—even with rocks sold as pre-cured—and that die-off can produce a lot of ammonia. All live rock must be fully cured in a separate container before it's safe to introduce it to your display tank.

Losing Part of Your Biofilter

Sometimes an ammonia spike happens not because you've increased the level of dissolved pollutants in your aquarium water but because part of the biofilter has been removed from the system. This can occur when you remove some of the rockwork or replace a mechanical filter medium (such as sponge or floss) or a chemical filter medium (such as activated carbon) that has been left in the aquarium long enough to become colonized by nitrifying bacteria. Mechanical and chemical filter media should be replaced at regular, frequent intervals to prevent this scenario.

A power outage is another way to lose biofiltration capacity, especially if your system includes a wet-dry biofilter. When the power goes out, water stops trickling over the biofilter medium, preventing the colonies of

This cowfish, Lactoria cornuta, *is a large and fascinating animal but not at all suited to a beginner's aquarium due to its size and toxic nature. Make sure you research any fish before acquiring it.*

nitrifying bacteria from doing their job, so the bacterial colonies soon begin to die off, and ammonia soon begins to build up in the tank. The use of an uninterrupted power supply (UPS) is a good way to keep your filtration going during a power failure. Otherwise, you may need to pour aquarium water down through your wet-dry filter at regular intervals until the power comes back on.

When Nitrate and Phosphate Accumulate

In the closed system of the aquarium, it's the invisible accumulation of compounds such as nitrate and phosphate that can cause some of the most frustrating problems. While not directly harmful to fish at low to moderate levels, these compounds function as fertilizer for various forms of algae—including the dreaded hair algae—and contribute to unsightly, smothering algae blooms if their levels aren't controlled.

How Does Nitrate Get in There?

As we've already established, nitrate is the end product of the nitrification process. As long as you've got a mature biofilter doing its job, you've got nitrate accumulating in your water. Nitrate can also enter the system via unpurified tap water and is present in some synthetic salt mixes. Nitrate is not harmful to fish at lower levels but should be kept as close to zero as possible. It is generally recommended that the nitrate level in a fish-only system be kept below 40 ppm, but a much lower reading—as close to undetectable as possible—is desired if you want to limit algae growth.

How Does Phosphate Get in There?

Phosphate is present in all living things, so it is introduced through feeding, the waste products of fish and other organisms, and the decomposition of organic matter. Phosphate may also be present in unpurified tap water as well as in some aquarium additives and synthetic salt mixes. Ideally, the phosphate level in your aquarium should not exceed 1 milligram per liter.

Playing Nitrate/Phosphate Detective

Test kits are available for monitoring the levels of both of these compounds, so if an algae problem arises, test your water to determine whether one (or both) of these compounds is accumulating to undesirable levels. If testing indicates that the level of one of these compounds is elevated, it's time to do some detective work to figure out the source.

Test your tap water to make sure you're not introducing these compounds with each water change or freshwater top-off, and check your salt mix to verify that it's nitrate- and phosphate-free. You'll also want to evaluate your stocking and feeding methods, as well as your filtration and tank maintenance techniques to ensure that you're doing everything possible to reduce the level of dissolved pollutants.

But I'm Using RO/DI!

If you're already purifying your tap water with an RO/DI system, you shouldn't have to worry about your tap water being the source for these compounds, right? Well, that's true only if your RO/DI system is properly

Don't Feed More Than They Need!

Children love to watch fish eat, so they may be tempted to feed the fish every time they look at the aquarium. Explain to them that feeding too much or too often will make the fish sick and pollute their water.

maintained. Don't forget that the various filtration media and the RO membrane must be replaced according to the manufacturer's recommendations if the system is to do its job efficiently.

Stock and Feed Lightly

Overstocking and overfeeding are among the biggest offenders when it comes to elevated nitrate and phosphate levels. The heavier the bioload, the more phosphate that is introduced and the more nitrate your biofilter will produce—assuming it can even keep pace with the dissolved pollutants. As we've already emphasized, your stocking rate should never exceed your aquarium's carrying capacity.

When feeding, be conscientious about portions and diligent about removing uneaten food from the system. Smaller portions fed more frequently are preferable to larger, infrequent feedings. Also, avoid adding the liquid that accompanies thawed frozen foods to your aquarium when feeding. To keep this major pollutant out of your system, strain and rinse the thawed portion of food over your sink in a fish net before feeding.

Chemical Filtration Helps!

Chemical filtration with activated carbon helps control nitrate levels by removing dissolved organic compounds from the water before they decompose and undergo biological

Some aquarists grow macroalgae, such as this Caulerpa *sp., to absorb excess nutrients in the water.*

filtration—which has nitrate as its end product.

Activated carbon is a material, such as wood, coal, or even coconut shell, that has been "activated" by baking at extremely high temperatures. Baking makes the material highly porous and alters its chemistry so that molecules of dissolved organic compounds form a bond with the surface of the carbon. This process, called adsorption, effectively removes the dissolved compounds from the water.

Ideally, activated carbon should be placed in an area where water flows

Other Chemical Filtration Media

Another line of defense against the buildup of nitrate or phosphate is available in the form of various resins and granular chemical filter media that are designed to specifically adsorb these compounds. While these products may live up to their claims, they do have their limitations. Specifically, they don't take into account the fact that the excessive accumulation of nitrate and/or phosphate signifies a decline in overall water quality that can't be remedied simply by cherry picking these compounds. Hence, you can't rely on these products exclusively for maintaining a high level of water quality.

Invest in a Protein Skimmer

If there's one water-purification device that no marine aquarium should be without, it's the protein skimmer. Next to the water change, there is no better method than protein skimming for removing dissolved organic compounds from the water before they can be acted upon by nitrifying bacteria.

Many variations on the protein skimmer design are available, but they all work by injecting a large volume of air bubbles—via a venturi valve or an airstone—into a chamber filled with water. As the tiny bubbles rise through the water column, molecules of dissolved organic compounds adhere to the bubbles and are carried to the top of the skimmer chamber, where they form

directly through it, and most filtration systems, including canister and hang-on-tank systems, are designed to accommodate this. However, you can also place a pouch of it in an overflow chamber or down in your sump.

Over time, activated carbon will become exhausted once it has adsorbed all of the dissolved pollutants it can hold. At that point, it must be replaced. The useful lifespan of activated carbon varies depending on the aquarium's bioload, but you can safely assume it should be replaced at least every six weeks to two months.

a thick, brown foam. As the foam builds, it rises up into a collection cup located at the top of the skimmer. There, the foam collapses into a nasty brown liquid. The aquarist then empties the collection cup, thereby eliminating the dissolved pollutants from the aquarium system.

A Change Will Do You Good!

The very best way to keep nitrate and phosphate levels in check is to perform routine partial water changes using purified tap water and a nitrate- and phosphate-free salt mix. If you stock sensibly, feed appropriately, utilize a protein skimmer, and change a portion of your aquarium water at regular intervals, elevated nitrate and phosphate levels should not become a problem in your aquarium. Read on to learn more about the invaluable water change!

The Great Equalizer: The Water Change

No amount of costly, high-tech equipment can replace the water change when it comes to maintaining exceptional water quality. Not only do water changes dilute nitrate, phosphate, and other dissolved pollutants, they also replenish the various trace elements that are vital to the health of marine life. In other words, water changes remove the bad stuff, replenish the good stuff, and help keep everything in balance.

What Are the Desired Volume and Frequency?

A good target amount for water changes is at least 20 percent of your aquarium volume each month—and more is even better. That doesn't necessarily mean that one 20-percent water change per month is ideal. Smaller, more frequent changes are preferable because they help to promote the stability of water parameters. A better regimen might be to do a 10-percent change every other week or a 5-percent change once a week. Of course, if your tank is supporting a relatively heavy bioload, larger, more frequent water changes would be appropriate.

Prepare the Water

Assuming you'll be using RO/DI-purified water for your water change, you'll need to start preparing your water a few days ahead

Activated Carbon and Phosphate Leaching

Low-quality activated carbon can actually leach excessive phosphate into your aquarium water! To check your chosen brand of carbon, add a teaspoonful of the carbon to a gallon of water, allow it to sit for about an hour, and then test the water for phosphate.

of your planned water change. Your RO/DI product water must be

The foam collected by your protein skimmer will condense in the cup as a thick brown liquid. This gunk consists of pollutants removed before they could degrade water quality.

aerated with a powerhead for about 24 hours after it is produced, in order to raise its dissolved oxygen level and "drive off" dissolved carbon dioxide, which can deplete the buffers in your salt mix. The water will also need to be heated to the same temperature as your aquarium water (in the range of 75° to 80°F [24° to 27°C]) with a small submersible heater.

Mix It Up

Next, mix in synthetic sea salt until you reach the desired specific gravity. Continue aerating your replacement water for another 24 hours to ensure that the salt has dissolved completely. Then, measure specific gravity again to make sure the value hasn't changed. Add more salt or purified water to the mix as needed, based on your hydrometer reading.

Mother Nature's Protein Skimmer

The foam that collects on an ocean beach on a windy day or that accumulates on the beach near areas of heavy surf is an example of natural protein skimming.

Shut Down the System

Before removing any water from the aquarium, unplug your heater and allow it to cool for about 15 minutes so it won't shatter in the event that it becomes exposed to air. Also, unplug your filtration system and powerheads. If you prefer, you can leave the lights on to help you see what you're doing during the water change.

Clean It Up

If the glass panes or rockwork of your aquarium are overgrown with algae, go ahead and clean them with an algae magnet (for the glass) and brush (for the rocks) at this point so that you can vacuum up any dislodged algae and other debris as you siphon out water.

A good way to ensure that you capture as much floating algae as possible is to attach a toothbrush to the wide end of your vacuum hose with a tie wrap so that any algae that you dislodge is immediately siphoned out of the tank. Use a turkey baster to liberate detritus that has collected on and around the rockwork, and then siphon away the suspended matter. Also, give your substrate the once-over with your vacuum hose to remove any detritus that has settled into it.

Starting the Siphon—the Hygienic Way

There's no need to suck on the end of your vacuum hose to get the siphon flowing. There's an easier—and much more hygienic—method. Simply place your waste-water bucket on the floor next to your tank, place the narrow end of your vacuum hose down in the bucket, and then lower the wide end of the hose, with the opening pointed up, into your aquarium. Once the wide end fills with water, slowly raise it out of the tank, with the open end still pointing up, and allow the water to begin running down through the hose into the bucket. Before all the water drains from the vacuum end, lower it down into the water again. At this point, a continuous siphon should be created (it may take a few tries), and you can go ahead and vacuum the tank.

When you're ready to stop—that is, once you've siphoned out a volume of

water equal to the volume of your replacement water—simply raise the vacuum out of the water with the open end pointing down to break the siphon.

Add Your Replacement Water

Now it's just a matter of adding your replacement water to the tank and plugging everything back in. Before emptying your waste water, use it to rinse trapped debris out of any sponges or other mechanical filtration media. Then, voila, your water change is done!

Temperature's Rising (or Falling)!

Many factors can influence the temperature of your aquarium water,

> *Regular water changes do more good for your tank that any chemical or piece of equipment.*

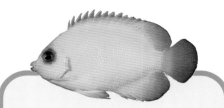

causing it to rise above or fall below your chosen setting within the desired range of 75° to 80°F (24° to 27°C). The biggest problems with water temperature swings tend to arise in regions that experience significant air temperature changes from one season to the next, but several other factors not related to seasonal change can come into play, as well.

Heater Malfunction

The first thing you'll need to rule out is whether your heater is malfunctioning or not. The indicator light can tell you a lot here. If the air temperature in your aquarium room is lower than the temperature at which you've set your heater thermostat, the light should be cycling on and off as the heater works to maintain the desired temperature. If it isn't turning on at all, either the heater is malfunctioning or you've set the thermostat too low (check it). On the other hand, if the indicator light stays on all the time, your heater may be broken or is too small for the size of your aquarium.

Don't Vacuum Fine Sand

Avoid vacuuming the substrate if it consists of fine sand, which will end up getting sucked right through your vacuum hose and out of your tank!

No Air Conditioning

In a home with no air conditioning, seasonal air temperature fluctuations (such as those that often occur in spring and autumn, when it can get hot in the day but cold at night) lead to pronounced aquarium water temperature fluctuations, especially in smaller tanks. But, if your home has central air conditioning or you've installed a window AC unit in the room where your aquarium is located, these fluctuations can be minimized by

Two Heaters Are Better Then One

As a hedge against plummeting temperatures in the event of a heater failure, many aquarists prefer to use two heaters rated at half the necessary wattage. So, rather than use a single 200-watt unit, they use two 100-watt units. By positioning the two heaters at opposite ends of the tank, you can also achieve better heat distribution throughout the system.

sunlight when you set up your tank actually bathes your tank with its lovely golden rays—and drives up the water temperature—at other times of year. If this situation is the cause of your problem, the remedy is simple. Cover the window with curtains, drapes, blinds, or a shade.

Look at Your Aquarium Lighting

The lights you use to illuminate your aquarium also produce heat, which can raise your water temperature. While this isn't a big problem with normal-output fluorescent bulbs, it can be a major aggravation for reef keepers who use high-intensity lighting, such as metal halide lamps or numerous very-high-output (VHO) fluorescent tubes, to illuminate their corals.

To prevent your lighting from causing a heat buildup, position a small fan to blow air across the surface of the water, which reduces the water temperature through evaporative cooling. Many aquarium lighting hoods have such fans built right in. Absent the built-in kind, you can always position a floor fan so that it blows across the top of your aquarium. Keep in mind, however, that using a fan will also increase the rate at which water evaporates from your tank, so you'll likely need to add more fresh water with each top-off.

Regularly vacuuming your substrate will remove trapped debris before it can decompose and pollute your water.

setting the AC thermostat within the desired range.

Look on the Bright Side

In Chapter 1, we discussed the importance of placing your aquarium away from sunny windows and other sources of heat or cold. However, the sun's position changes throughout the year, so it's possible to discover that a window that wasn't letting in much

Got Watts?

For an aquarium heater to do its job properly, it must be of the correct wattage for the size of your aquarium. If the wattage is too low, the heater will constantly struggle to maintain the set temperature or will fall short of reaching it when the ambient air temperature is relatively low. On the other hand, if the wattage is too high for your needs, you'll be constantly fighting elevated water temperatures.

Fortunately, it's usually easy to determine the proper wattage for any given size of aquarium because heater manufacturers typically include this information right on their product packaging. If this information isn't provided on the heater package, use the formula of 3 to 5 watts per gallon of aquarium water to get in the right ballpark. So, for a 55-gallon (200-liter) tank, you would need between 165 and 275 watts of heating power, depending on how cool you keep the room in which your aquarium is located.

Should You Chill Out?

If your home lacks air conditioning and you're facing some steamy summer temperatures, your best option for keeping your aquarium's water temperature within the desired range may be to invest in a chiller unit. With a chiller, aquarium water is pumped through a heat exchanger, which is charged with a compressed refrigerant, then returned to the tank at a lower temperature. The only drawback to these units is that they can be costly, so the hobbyist on a limited budget may want to exhaust all other cooling options first.

Make sure you have the appropriate lighting for the size of your tank. Overdoing it will drive up your water temperature.

Chapter 4

Behavior and Compatibility

Concerns Solved

Having the opportunity to observe and enjoy the beauty and fascinating behavior of marine life is what draws most people to the saltwater aquarium hobby. Sometimes, though, the hair-raising way our aquatic charges behave or interact with one another is enough to make us think that, perhaps, we should have taken up golf instead! But, armed with the right knowledge, you'll be able to overcome most marine life misbehavior and compatibility quandaries.

When Fish Won't Feed

Getting fish to eat would seem to be one of the easiest aspects of our hobby. After all, fish need to eat in order to survive, so once they get hungry enough, they'll eat whatever we offer them, right? Well, unfortunately, it's not always that simple. Some can be remarkably stubborn when it comes to eating in the aquarium, while others will never learn to accept the foods we offer.

No Thanks, I'm Not Hungry!

When fish are first introduced to an aquarium, it's not at all unusual for them to forgo eating for a time—sometimes an alarmingly long time—while they get acclimated to their new surroundings. This is usually not a cause for concern.

Fish can go for many days, or even weeks, without eating with no harm done. Just keep offering a variety of foods (be sure to regularly siphon out any uneaten items), and your reluctant feeder should eventually become more confident and start sampling the foods you present. Chopped fresh clams are a great food for enticing reluctant feeders. Few fish can resist their allure for long!

You Call This Food?

Remember, most of the fish in the saltwater aquarium trade are still wild-caught. What they're accustomed to eating on the natural coral reefs bears

Despite what you may hear or read, lionfish should not be fed goldfish, as they are nutritionally deficient.

Though beautiful, the splendid leopard wrasse, Macropharyngodon bipartitus, *has a highly specialized diet and they almost always starve to death. Fortunately, many other wrasses are much easier to wean to a captive diet.*

little resemblance to the chunks, strips, pellets, and flakes we tend to feed them in captivity—even if these items are perfectly sound from the standpoint of nutrition. While some species will take to these offerings almost immediately, others may need a little more convincing.

Some Like it Live

Some fish require live foods, such as feeder fish or live crustaceans, to initiate a feeding response in the aquarium. Trouble is, it's impractical at best to feed live foods to our fish for the long term. In the case of feeder fish, it can be downright unhealthy, as these typically starved specimens have little nutritional value and can also introduce disease to your aquarium. Therefore, it's a good idea to wean fish off live foods as soon as possible.

Weaning From Live Foods

To accomplish this, start introducing non-living foods along with the live offerings. The more closely the non-living food resembles the living food the better. In fact, your best bet is to begin by offering non-living versions of the same food. For example, if you've been feeding live mysid shrimp, start substituting frozen mysid shrimp. In the frenzy of feeding, some of the non-living food will be consumed along with the live food. Over consecutive feedings, keep increasing the amount of non-live foods while tapering off the live foods until they're phased out completely. Then, if you want to introduce flake, pellet, or freeze-dried foods, you can begin to present these foods along with the frozen mysid shrimp, which the fish has already come to accept.

The Specialized Feeder

Some fish have such specialized diets that they will never learn to accept aquarium foods, no matter how persistent you are. For example, many butterflyfishes, such as the aptly named exquisite butterflyfish, *Chaetodon austriacus*, are obligate corallivores, which is a fancy way of saying they eat live coral polyps and nothing else. Unless you are able to provide a steady supply of live coral for these fish, they have no place in your aquarium. Always research the dietary needs of any specimen—and make sure you can provide for them over the life of the specimen—before you buy it.

First Night Jitters

In nature, when a fish is startled or pursued, it can attempt to flee in virtually any direction. It can even leap right out of the water to escape a predator's line of sight.

When a fish tries to escape a threat in the confines of an aquarium, however, it may end up leaping right out of the tank and landing on the fishroom floor, where its death is assured unless the hobbyist is close at hand to intervene.

Any fish can jump, and this is most likely to occur right after lights out on the day the fish is introduced to the aquarium. Why are fish so skittish that first night? Well, you'd be nervous too if someone locked you up in a room full of strangers and suddenly turned out the lights. Besides, on the coral reefs, a lot of hungry predators begin cruising in search of a meal right after dark, and a newly introduced fish hasn't had much time to locate a safe retreat.

Territorial Tankmates

Harassment by more aggressive tankmates can also drive fish to leap out of the frying pan and into the fire. This can be a concern for both newly introduced and established specimens that have become the target of a tankmate's territorial aggression.

Hawkfishes are just one of the species of fish that may be itching to jump right out of your tank.

"Marine Houdinis"

While all fish can jump, some, such as firefishes, hawkfishes, anthias, and grammas, are more prone to this behavior than others. Some fish, such as moray eels, are notorious escape artists that will attempt to liberate themselves from any confined space whether they're frightened or merely curious. Special precautions must be taken to ensure that these marine Houdinis can't find an easy way out.

Put a Lid on It and Look for the Problem!

Your best line of defense against this fatal form of fish acrobatics is to cover your aquarium with a tight-fitting sheet (or sheets) of glass or acrylic. Keep any openings for accommodating tubes, hoses, heaters, filter returns, or other equipment as narrow as possible, as even small gaps in the cover can serve as an escape hatch for the determined jumper.

Of course, if fish jumping from your tank is actually a symptom of poor water quality, you can't just put a lid on your tank and call it a day! You'll need to take the necessary steps to correct the problem that's degrading your water conditions. The same is true of excessive tankmate aggression. The solution here is not just to prevent the victim's escape but to find a way to stop the aggressive behavior. The next section of this chapter will give you some pointers

Let Me Out!

If something's amiss with your water conditions, your fish may attempt to find cleaner pastures by jumping out of the tank. This is why it's so important to keep your aquarium as clean as possible.

for minimizing aggression among your fish.

Don't Flush That Jumper Just Yet!

It's heartbreaking to discover too late that a fish has leapt from the tank and dried out on the floor. But don't assume right away that it is too late! Even if the fish has begun to dry out, you might still be able to revive it by placing it in a bowl or bucket filled with water from your aquarium. Gently move the fish forward and backward so water flows over its gills. Many a presumed-dead specimen has been brought back from the brink in this manner. Besides, you've got nothing to lose if you try.

Behavior and Compatibility Concerns Solved

Carefully researching the fish you decide to buy will allow you to create a peaceful tank.

Dealing with Egregious Aggression

Competition for territory and resources is extremely fierce on the coral reef, and many fish will use aggression to drive off intruders and protect what is rightfully theirs. When you take several fish accustomed to occupying and defending relatively large areas of reef and put them together within the confines of an aquarium (even the biggest tank is pretty small compared to the natural coral reefs), it should come as no surprise that some territorial disputes are inevitable. The good news is that, if you do your homework before buying and introduce livestock thoughtfully, your saltwater aquarium doesn't have to become an underwater war zone.

Research, Research, Research!

Before purchasing a single specimen, it's critical to research the temperaments (not to mention the care requirements) of the fish you'd like to include in your aquarium. If you purchase fishes simply because they're pretty or exotic-looking with no thought given to their behavior, you're headed for serious trouble. Why? Consider the following:

• Some fish, such as certain triggerfishes, are far too aggressive or unpredictable for the community tank and are best suited for a single-specimen tank.

• Most fish, even relatively peaceful herbivores, will not turn down the opportunity to gobble up a tankmate that is small enough to fit in their mouths.

- Some smaller fish, including many dottybacks and damsels, can be extraordinarily aggressive toward tankmates—even those many times their own size.
- Some fishes should be kept only by themselves or with tankmates of similar size and aggressiveness.
- Some fish—again, certain triggerfishes come to mind—have a reputation for being good community tank citizens at first and then suddenly deciding to go on a rampage against their tankmates.

As these points suggest, choosing a combination of fishes based on looks alone could have disastrous consequences!

Attacking the Newcomer

A new specimen introduced to a tank that already contains an established population is often a target for aggression—especially if the newcomer is naturally more passive than others in the community—and may be subjected to relentless attacks.

In this case, it can be helpful to rearrange the rockwork or decorations in the aquarium before introducing the new fish. This "reshuffling of the deck" essentially erases all the existing territorial boundaries, so the resident fishes are more inclined to focus their attention on establishing new territories rather than attacking the newcomer. In essence, it puts all the fishes on a level playing field.

As an alternative, or in addition to this method, remove the more aggressive fishes from the display tank, house them temporarily in your quarantine tank, and then reintroduce them after the new fish has had a chance to settle in.

The One-To-a-Tank Rule

Many saltwater fishes gather in spectacular schools in nature, and it can be very tempting to try to recreate this effect in the aquarium. Unfortunately, keeping more than one specimen of a given species seldom works out as envisioned. Reef fishes, even those that school, can be very territorial toward their

The Meek Shall Inherit the Tank...At First

When stocking your tank with fish, always introduce species according to their level of aggressiveness, with the least aggressive species being introduced first and the most aggressive being introduced last. That way, the more passive species will have an opportunity to establish themselves before the scrappier species come along.

own kind. After all, members of the same species present the most direct competition for resources.

Some species can be successfully kept more than one to a tank, provided all the specimens are introduced at the same time, the tank is fairly large, and the aquascaping allows the individuals to stay out of each other's line of sight. Exceptions can sometimes be made in the case of fish that are sold as mated pairs, as well. However, as a general rule, it's best to keep only one individual of a species per tank.

Familiarity Breeds Contempt

Not only do you have to be careful about keeping more than one individual of a species in the same tank, but you also must proceed with caution when it comes to housing individuals of different species that are very similar in appearance, have the same diet, or

occupy the same ecological niche on the reef, as each may view the other as a competitor. This is often a problem when keeping different species from the same genus. But it can also occur between completely unrelated species that have evolved similar physical characteristics or habits.

Come Out, Come Out!

You're doing your daily head count of the fish in your tank when you notice that a specimen is unaccounted for. Your first thought is that the fish has jumped from the tank, but a careful scan of the entire floor surrounding the aquarium reveals nothing. Could the fish have vanished into thin air? Well, it may seem like it, but fish can evade our detection in a variety of

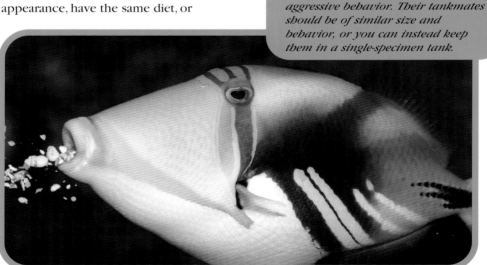

Triggerfish can display highly aggressive behavior. Their tankmates should be of similar size and behavior, or you can instead keep them in a single-specimen tank.

Royal grammas, Gramma loreto, *cannot be kept together. Limit one to a tank.*

ways. The specimen may be right under your nose and you just don't realize it.

First, Rule Out a Fatality

If the missing fish has died and is hidden within the rockwork, you'll need to conduct your recovery mission promptly and remove it from the system before it decomposes and possibly causes an ammonia spike.

Buried Alive

Many fish have evolved fascinating behaviors that allow them to conceal themselves from predators at night or whenever they feel frightened or threatened. One such behavior is burying in the substrate. Fish that exhibit this, including many wrasses, can give their keepers palpitations because they seemingly vanish from sight when they're actually just hidden in the sand. Incidentally, most wrasses are good jumpers, too, so these fish can do a disappearing act in more ways than one!

The Shy Type

Some fish, such as the comet (a.k.a. the marine betta), *Calloplesiops altivelis,* are just timid by nature and can't be expected to swim out of hiding whenever the hobbyist approaches the tank. Therefore, a vanishing act by one of these fish is perfectly normal. Shy fish need ample nooks and caves to hide in and give them a sense of security. Ironically, if timid species have lots of places to hide nearby, they'll actually be more inclined to spend time out in the open.

Victim of Harassment

A fish that is constantly chased and harassed by a more aggressive specimen may seek refuge in the rockwork and remain there to avoid drawing the attention of its antagonistic tankmate. If you observe one fish constantly tormenting another, and none of the steps described earlier for minimizing aggression (i.e., rearranging the tank decor or removing and reintroducing the aggressor) seem to make a difference, you'll need to permanently remove either the aggressor or its victim from the aquarium to restore peace.

Seeing Double?

First-time keepers of ornamental shrimp, crabs, and other crustaceans often go through an upsetting initiation. They make the shocking discovery of what appears to be the deceased body of their valued crustacean somewhere in the tank. But more often than not, what they're actually seeing is an exoskeleton that has just been molted by the crustacean. The animal itself is usually in hiding somewhere in the rocks while its soft, new exoskeleton hardens. Although alarming when observed for the first time, this behavior is perfectly normal and necessary, as a crustacean's exoskeleton does not increase in size along with the animal and must be shed to allow for continued growth.

Failure to Molt

On the other hand, there are circumstances in which crustaceans either fail to molt or molt incompletely, and this is usually fatal to the animal. Low iodine levels are often the suspected cause in these instances. While iodine supplements are available, you must proceed with caution if you choose to dose iodine directly into your aquarium, as it is very easy to overdose. Never dose iodine indiscriminately or without testing!

A better way to restore and maintain a sufficient iodine level is to perform

SMALL FRY

Why Do They Sell Them, Then?

Shopping for fish is a great opportunity to teach kids that not all species sold in stores are good choices for the home aquarium—no matter how pretty they might be. Some won't eat the foods we offer, some get way too big, some are too aggressive, and so on. Point out species that have a bad survival record in captivity and explain why they should have been left on the reef.

water changes using a quality synthetic sea salt. Iodine is in the salt mix in the proper proportions—along with other trace elements that likely play an important role in the molting process.

Catch Me if You Can!

Removing a trouble-making fish from an established aquarium is a chore much easier said than done, especially in larger, heavily aquascaped tanks. In such systems, it may seem that the only option is to pull out all of the rockwork until there's nothing left for the fish to hide under and then chase it

down with a net. But before resorting to such drastic measures, you can try several less destructive techniques that just might bring the errant fish to heel.

Divide and Conquer

If your tank is more sparsely aquascaped on one side, try to encourage the fish to take refuge on that side and then insert a tank divider to block the fish's retreat. Then, you can remove its hiding places and net out the fish. While still somewhat disruptive, this technique at least minimizes the amount of disassembling and reassembling of rockwork that is necessary.

Try Traps

For smaller fish, baited traps can be an effective, and far less disruptive, method of capture. Commercially manufactured acrylic traps are available for this purpose. Or, you can try one of several do-it-yourself designs.

One of the most commonly recommended DIY traps is made from a transparent two-liter soda bottle. After thoroughly rinsing, cut off the top third of the bottle. Take the third that you cut off and invert it into the bottle so that the narrow end now points toward the bottom of the bottle. Use a few dabs of aquarium-safe silicone to secure the top in place. Next, put some food in the bottle for bait, place the bottle on its side down in the tank, and wait.

Patience will be your greatest ally with any trapping technique, as it usually takes time for a fish to become accustomed to the presence of the trap and even consider venturing in. Also, Murphy's Law being in effect here, don't be surprised if you catch every other specimen in your tank before the target fish takes the bait.

Lower the Level

One of the biggest challenges of capturing a feisty fish is that it can escape your net in three dimensions. If you drain the aquarium water into another vessel until it's just deep enough for the fish to stay submerged, you'll find that you and your fish are on a much more level playing field, and netting the specimen will be significantly easier. Once the fish is caught, promptly restore the water level in the aquarium.

Hook and Line

It may seem like using a jackhammer to drive a nail, but sometimes the most effective way to catch and remove a larger fish is to use a fishing line with a baited hook. To minimize the potential for injury to the fish, first file down the barb on the hook. Keep in mind, however, that once the fish is caught, it will thrash about, so using this technique to capture a venomous or spiny species could result in serious injury and is not recommended.

Chapter 5

Plagues, Pests, and

Uninvited Guests

Up until now, we've focused on the challenges associated with creating a suitable, stable, and peaceful habitat for the marine life that we want to keep alive and thriving in our tanks. But what about the living things that we *don't* want in our tanks—the various troublesome algae and pests that sometimes reach plague proportions in aquariums? Is there a way to prevent these uninvited guests from taking up residence, or to evict them once they've arrived?

Part of the Coral Reef Web of Life

Before we look at the different troublesome organisms that you might encounter, it's important to understand that all of the organisms discussed in this chapter, no matter how irksome, are just as much a part of the natural coral reef as the beautiful fish and corals are. On the reefs, their growth is kept in balance thanks to the incredible diversity of grazers and predators, as well as the limited availability of dissolved nutrients. In the aquarium, where few natural controls are present, however, they can quickly get out of hand.

A Progression of Algae

As your aquarium matures after setup and cycling, you can expect your tank to undergo a progression of algae blooms, which includes diatoms, cyanobacteria, and green hair algae (incidentally, these are not all "true" algae, but to keep things simple, we'll treat them all as such here). While each bloom can be quite ugly and discouraging, this series of blooms is a perfectly normal process, and each form of alga will eventually dissipate once the nutrients it needs for survival are used up.

But, if you overfeed, overstock, or fail to keep dissolved nutrients low through vigorous protein skimming and routine aquarium maintenance (water changes!), these algae can come back at any time—and with a vengeance.

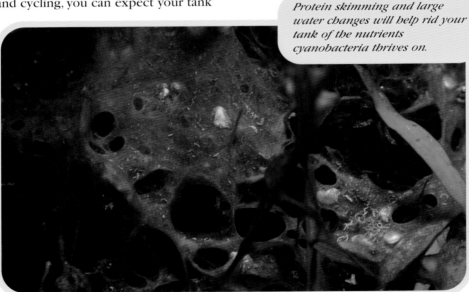

Protein skimming and large water changes will help rid your tank of the nutrients cyanobacteria thrives on.

A Dusting of Diatoms

Diatoms typically appear as a dusting of golden brown all over the aquarium glass, rocks, and other surfaces, but when conditions are right, that growth can become quite excessive. Diatom growth is usually caused by elevated silicate levels. Silicate is an important element that is found in natural sea water, but it can become a problem when a higher-than-normal level is reached due to the use of unpurified tap water, certain salt mixes, or a silica sand substrate.

If you're using RO/DI-purified source water for top-offs and water changes, you should be able to eliminate your tap water as a potential source of silicate. Also, make sure your salt mix does not contain a higher-than-normal level of silicate. Your substrate, if you choose to include one, should consist of a calcium-based material, such as aragonite, rather than silica sand.

Slimy Cyanobacteria

Better known as slime algae or blue-green algae, cyanobacteria form a slimy red, black, or green coating on the rocks and substrate, especially in areas of low water flow. If cyanobacteria growth gets bad enough, you might even see rafts of the stuff bubbling up from the substrate to the surface of the tank.

To eradicate this nuisance, you'll need to cut off its nutrient supply through protein skimming and water changes, as well as by stepping up the

Antibiotics and Cyanobacteria

Antibiotics can be used to kill cyanobacteria, but this is not the best course of action since antibiotics can also wipe out the beneficial nitrifying bacteria that make up your biofilter. Besides, the use of antibiotics merely treats the symptom of cyanobacteria growth. It doesn't address the underlying water-quality problem that caused the bloom in the first place.

water movement in affected areas. Cyanobacteria tend to be loosely attached, so when performing water changes, try to siphon out as much of the slimy stuff as you can.

Pulling Your Hair Out Over Hair Algae?

Hair algae is a blanket term for several species of filamentous green algae that can take hold in a tank whenever dissolved nutrients and ample lighting are present. In contrast to cyanobacteria, hair algae tend to favor areas of brisk water movement. When conditions favor the growth of these pesky algae, they can spread to the point of completely overgrowing the tank.

In addition to starving out hair algae through protein skimming, water changes, and the use of purified tap water, it's helpful to pull as much of the yucky green stuff out by hand as you can. You can also use a toothbrush (preferably not one you're still using for your teeth!) to scrub the algae off the rockwork. Just be sure to siphon out any clumps that you dislodge so they don't drift to other parts of the tank and take hold.

Don't Burst Your Bubbles!

One form of alga that is often transported into aquariums on live rock is actually quite interesting and, some might argue, quite attractive—bubble alga. As the name suggests, bubble alga looks like green to silvery-green bubbles, ranging in size from approximately that of a pea to about the size of a silver dollar. Trouble is, those pretty little bubbles can rapidly overgrow an aquarium.

Your best bet for getting rid of bubble alga is to pick out the bubbles by hand whenever you notice one. To do this, gently grasp the bubble between your thumb and forefinger and carefully wiggle it until it comes loose. Take care not to burst the bubble in the process as this will release all the tiny spores contained within the bubble and create an even bigger problem than you started with.

Limit the Light

Along with dissolved nutrients to serve as fertilizer, many forms of nuisance algae need ample light to thrive. While it's not practical to eliminate light completely (for aquarists who maintain photosynthetic invertebrates, this would be a really bad idea), you should not leave your lights on any longer than necessary. For fish-only systems, six to eight hours of light per day is sufficient. To make sure you don't leave your lights on too long, put your fixture on a timer so it turns on and off on schedule every day. Of course, if sunlight from a nearby window is contributing to the problem, you'll need to cover the window to keep the light from reaching your tank.

Algae-Munching Critters

Herbivorous organisms can be an important ally in your battle against

Be careful when plucking bubble algae. Rupturing one will lead to more algae in your tank.

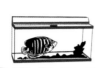

Algae as a Teaching Tool

An algae outbreak provides a great environmental lesson for children. Explain to them how excessive pollutants in the water can cause algae blooms that smother coral reefs. Show them the important role herbivorous animals play in keeping algae growth in control.

nuisance algae. These can include herbivorous fish, such as tangs and rabbitfishes, as well as various algae-munching snails and crustaceans. In fact, large numbers of snails and hermit crabs are often packaged together and sold as cleanup crews. Emerald, or Mithrax, crabs are commonly sold for combating bubble algae. These various critters sometimes do their job really well, but sometimes they just don't live up to expectation. Results will vary!

Is One More One Too Many?

Keep in mind that any time you add an animal to the system—even for a practical purpose such as algae control—you are increasing your aquarium's bioload and introducing

more dissolved pollutants. That means you might actually be contributing to the very problem you're trying to control. Depending on how heavily stocked your tank is to begin with, adding just one more fish or a mess of snails and hermits could overwhelm your biofilter, leading to an ammonia spike.

Eating Themselves Out of House and Home

Furthermore, you must consider what will happen to the specimen once the form of alga it feeds upon is gone. For instance, while there are numerous options for feeding tangs and rabbitfishes beyond the algae growing in your tank, some snails will eat only one form of alga, such as diatoms; once they've eaten all the diatoms in your aquarium, the snails will starve to death unless they are promptly moved to another system containing a film of diatoms.

Fight Algae with Algae

Many advanced saltwater hobbyists have discovered that an excellent way to limit nuisance algae is to cultivate various desirable species of macroalgae in their systems. The macroalgae, which are usually grown in a refugium (a separate tank that shares water with the display tank), take up dissolved nutrients from the water, thereby starving out the nuisance algae. The nutrients taken up by the macroalgae are then exported—a fancy way of saying removed—from the system through regular pruning of the macroalgae.

Flatworm Infestation!

A flatworm, or planaria, infestation can easily sneak up on you because these little pests can be hard to spot. The type most familiar to aquarists, the rust brown flatworm, can easily blend in against a background of various coralline algae—that is, until the aquarist notices that those tiny patches of "algae" are actually moving. True to its name, this species is brown to rusty orange or red in color, is roughly oval shaped, and reaches about one-eighth to one-fourth of an inch (3 to 6 mm) in length.

These planaria can rapidly multiply to plague proportions, forming thick mats, generally in areas of minimal water movement. As with nuisance algae, these flatworms seem to thrive in tanks with excessive dissolved nutrients.

Although a severe flatworm infestation might seem to be cause for drastic measures, such outbreaks are usually self-limiting, with the population crashing as rapidly as it increased. To help hasten the population decline, take whatever steps are necessary to lower the dissolved pollutant level in your tank, including protein skimming, water changes (siphoning out as many of the worms as you can), and the use of activated carbon. Also, increase the water movement in your tank so that no dead spots are present.

Some fish, including certain wrasses and dragonets, as well as certain nudibranchs (sea slugs) are sometimes recommended for controlling flatworms, but this approach is hit-or-miss at best. Your best bet is to make the necessary environmental changes to improve water quality and movement.

What a Cute Little Anemone!

You've recently added some live rock or a coral specimen to your tank. A few days later you notice that a cute little anemone—sort of brownish and almost transparent—has appeared on one of the live rocks or on the rock or plug to which the coral is attached. At first, you think to yourself, "What a nice bonus!" But then your outlook begins to change when you realize that duplicates of the cute little

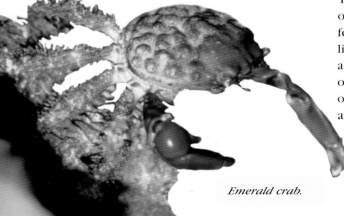

Emerald crab.

specimen are popping up everywhere at an alarming rate. You've got an outbreak of *Aiptasia*, a.k.a. glass anemones or rock anemones, on your hands!

Don't Panic!

Spotting a single specimen of *Aiptasia* is not a cause for panic. The solution may be as simple as removing the rock that the specimen is attached to from the tank and allowing it to dry out, which will kill the anemone. If these anemones have already begun to spread, there are many other actions you can take to bring them under control, and each method has its pros and cons.

Ways to Stick It to 'Em

Although the process can be painstaking, one of the techniques that can be successful in ridding a tank of *Aiptasia* is to inject each anemone with a caustic chemical or other product designed to kill these critters. Some options include:

- a concentrated solution of calcium hydroxide (known as kalkwasser or limewater)
- sodium hydroxide (highly caustic— handle with care!)
- concentrated lemon juice (among the safest methods and reportedly very effective)
- one of the various commercial products formulated for killing *Aiptasia*

When injecting any caustic chemical, it's best to treat small areas of the aquarium at a time. For best results, you'll need to inject each specimen using a hypodermic needle directly in its base, making sure the needle doesn't pass right through. The biggest challenge you'll face when using this technique is getting the anemones to stay expanded long enough to stick them with the needle. *Aiptasia* can vanish into tiny crevices in the rock with surprising speed.

Bring On the Butterflyfishes

Various species of butterflyfishes, such as the copperband butterflyfish, *Chelmon rostratus*; Klein's butterflyfish, *Chaetodon kleinii*; the raccoon butterflyfish, *Chaetodon lunula*; and others, have a fairly solid track record of eating *Aiptasia* in the aquarium. Then again, some individuals might not live up to this reputation.

If you decide to introduce a butterflyfish for *Aiptasia* control, make

Don't Go Medieval on *Aiptasia*!

Anemones spreading like wildfire? Time to dice and slice, right? Wrong! Ripping, tearing, chopping, or otherwise mutilating *Aiptasia* will only lead to more of these aggravating anemones, as new specimens can regenerate from even the tiniest shred of tissue.

Aiptasia *anemone.*

sure you're able to provide for its care requirements for the long term and that you've considered all possible compatibility issues with your current livestock.

Give 'Em a Taste of Peppermint!

The peppermint shrimp, which is an attractive and interesting aquarium inhabitant in its own right, is another known predator of *Aiptasia*. Don't rely on the common name when purchasing this species for *Aiptasia* control, however, as several similar-looking shrimp species are sold as "peppermint shrimp" but not all of them will eat *Aiptasia*. Be sure to ask for this species by its scientific name: *Lysmata wurdemanni.*

An Aiptasia-*Nibbling* Nudibranch

Yet another form of biological control for *Aiptasia* is a particular species of nudibranch, *Berghia verrucicornis.* This little sea slug eats only *Aiptasia*, which means it must be moved to a tank with more *Aiptasia* once it has exhausted the supply in your aquarium or else it will starve to death.

Yikes! Spiny Worms!

There's something about the sight of a long (sometimes really long!), spiky worm suddenly crawling out of the aquarium rockwork that just seems to fill people with a sense of disgust and a desire to get rid of the intruder at any cost.

So-called bristleworms typically make their entrance into the saltwater aquarium as live rock stowaways. These worms are named for the bristle-like spines lining their sides, which are sharp, brittle, and, in some cases, venomous. Depending on the species you come in contact with, it's possible to experience a skin reaction ranging from a rash to an intense, burning pain if you brush against one of these worms.

Chelmon rostratus

Guilt by Association

That being said, most bristleworms are actually beneficial in the aquarium, as they feed on detritus that builds up in the substrate. However, because there are a few nasty, carnivorous species, such as the notorious *Hermodice carunculata*, that have a reputation for feasting on invertebrates and dispensing nasty stings to aquarists, we tend to regard all similar-looking polychaete worms with equal suspicion.

Screen Your Live Rock

If you don't want to take the chance that one of the nasty bristleworm species will make it into your tank along with the benign kind, be sure to screen your live rock carefully before placing it in your tank. Right after you unpack the rocks, look them over carefully for bristleworms protruding from crevices or crawling on the surface. Protect your hands with

gloves and use tweezers to remove any that you see, wiggling them gently to dislodge them from their holes in the rocks.

Keep It Clean

Regularly vacuuming your substrate to keep it free of detritus—the primary source of nutrients for most of these worms—will help to limit the bristleworm population in your tank, as well.

What Eats Bristleworms?

As with most saltwater aquarium pests, there are various fishes and/or crustaceans that may help control bristleworms. These biological-control species include, among others, the coral-banded shrimp, *Stenopus hispidus*; the arrow crab, *Stenorhynchus seticornis*; and various wrasses.

Can You Trap Them?

Various commercial traps are available for catching bristleworms at night, when they tend to emerge from hiding and roam about. Or, you can use a homemade trap, such

Mantis shrimp are intelligent creatures that are best kept, if kept at all, in acrylic tanks.

as a glass pipette with bait at the closed end or a baited section of PVC pipe with holes drilled in it and the ends capped. You can even use a nylon stocking with a piece of bait placed inside it (men, please get your significant other's approval before raiding her stocking drawer!). As the bristleworms attempt to feed on the bait in the stocking, their spines will become ensnared in the nylon.

Marauding Mantis Shrimp

The mantis shrimp is another live rock hitchhiker that can become a big problem in saltwater aquaria. These cantankerous crustaceans, which bear a passing resemblance to the preying mantis insect because of the way they fold their feeding appendages against their body, can really wreak havoc on aquarium livestock, which they prey upon at night. Not actually true shrimps, which are placed in the order Decapoda, the mantis shrimp have their own order, Stomatopoda.

"Spearers" and "Smashers"

The design of mantis shrimp feeding appendages, called chelae, varies depending on the prey items the particular species tends to eat. The chelae of the so-called "spearers" are

blade-like with multiple barbs for stabbing soft-bodied prey, such as fish, while the chelae of the "smashers" are more club-like for smashing open exoskeletons and shells of crustaceans and mollusks. These chelae are capable of striking with staggering speed and, in the case of larger specimens, with sufficient force to break aquarium glass. These lethal chelae have also given rise to the mantis shrimp's nickname—"thumbsplitter"—which is used among various fisherfolk and live rock collectors who have gained firsthand knowledge of the injuries they can inflict on hapless humans.

Not All Are Equally Dangerous

Discovering a mantis shrimp in your tank doesn't necessarily mean you're dealing with one of the notorious thumbsplitters or tankbusters. There are literally hundreds of mantis shrimp species, and they range in adult size from less than an inch to over 12 inches (2 to 30 cm). Clearly, the threat posed by a one-inch (2.5-cm) specimen to both aquarium livestock and aquarists' fingers is significantly less than that posed by a foot-long specimen. Still, even the little ones can take their toll on smaller fishes, mollusks, and crustaceans.

Signs of a Mantis Shrimp

Because these crustaceans are nocturnal and very stealthy, they often go unnoticed until fishes and/or invertebrates begin to vanish overnight. Remnants of broken crustacean or mollusk shells that can't be blamed on any other livestock in the tank can also indicate the presence of a mantis shrimp. Many hobbyists who have discovered mantis shrimp in their systems report hearing a clicking sound at night, which is likely caused when the shrimp is clubbing a hard-shelled prey item or excavating inside the rock.

Flush It Out of Its Lair

If you can identify the specific rock the mantis shrimp is hiding in, getting rid of

it is a simple matter of removing the rock from your tank and flushing out the specimen. Getting the shrimp to abandon its lair can be accomplished in one of several ways:

- Squirt soda water directly into the hole it's hiding in or briefly submerge the entire rock in soda water.
- Dip the rock in fresh water.
- Pour boiling water into the shrimp's lair.

Or Set a Snare

If you can't tell which rock the mantis shrimp is holing up in or if you're dealing with more than one specimen, a baited trap might be your best option. There are various commercial traps to choose from, or you can try to make a trap yourself. The plastic soda bottle trap for catching fishes, which is described in Chapter 4, is also effective for catching mantis shrimp. A simple online search will yield lots of additional DIY trap designs, as well.

Savvy Shrimp

Mantis shrimp are pretty smart—as crustaceans go—so they can learn fairly quickly to avoid a trap. If one trap doesn't seem to be working, try switching to a different design.

Odontodactylus scyllarus, one of the many species of mantis shrimp.

Chapter 6

Equipment and Maintenance

Problems Solved

Success with a saltwater aquarium depends on keeping your equipment in good working order. Even the most low-tech system incorporates at least a few key pieces of equipment that are critical for maintaining marine organisms in good health. This chapter addresses many of the common equipment problems you might encounter and offers practical tips for preventing or remedying them.

Mechanical Filter Failure

Several problems can interfere with a mechanical filter, resulting in either a low flow rate or no flow whatsoever. Fortunately, most of these problems are easy to solve.

Low Flow

If water is flowing through your mechanical filter but at a reduced rate, first check to make sure the flow-control valve (if one is present) is opened to allow the desired level of water flow. If that's not the problem, examine the filter medium to make sure it isn't clogged with uneaten food, fish waste, and other gunk, which can cause the water to bypass the medium—a process known as channeling—so that it doesn't get filtered efficiently. Replace the clogged medium or, if it isn't too heavily encrusted, rinse it out in a bucket of aquarium water.

Also, make sure the slots in the filter's intake tube aren't clogged with debris and that the filter's impeller is able to spin freely. Impellers are notorious for becoming snarled with hair algae (or even human hair) or blocked by bits of substrate, activated carbon, or other debris. In addition, sticky gunk coating the inside of the intake tube can reduce water flow. To keep this buildup from occurring, you should routinely clean the intake tube or hose with an aquarium brush.

No Flow

When you plug in a mechanical filter and it simply fails to draw water—or perhaps it produces an unsettling chugging sound yet still fails to start flowing—the most likely problem is that you've forgotten to prime the filter or that the filter has lost its prime. Priming simply involves filling the filter compartments with water before starting the unit so that the pump is able to initiate and maintain water flow.

With hang-on-tank filters, priming simply involves filling the filter chamber with salt water before plugging it in. Canister filters, on the other hand, are usually equipped with

SMALL FRY

Not for Touching!

All the gizmos, gadgets, tubes, and cords located in and around a saltwater aquarium can be very enticing to curious little ones. But if a child plays with something he or she shouldn't, the results can be disastrous—to your fish, the floor, or even the child. Little kids must be taught that aquarium equipment is not for touching, especially when electricity is involved!

an integrated priming feature (a button you push to prime the unit), although older models lacked this feature. With older canister filters, priming involved sucking the air out of the filter components, either by mouth or using a special bulb device, so that aquarium water could flow in.

Loss of prime usually occurs as a result of a power failure or when the water level in the tank is allowed to drop (usually as a result of evaporation) to the point that the intake is exposed to air and the siphon is broken. Once the siphon breaks and water flow stops, the filter pump does not have the "oomph" to start it up again without being re-primed. To avoid this problem (as well as to prevent a major spike in specific gravity), simply keep your aquarium's water topped off at the appropriate level and be sure to re-prime the filter after a power outage.

A well-maintained protein skimmer will do wonders for your aquarium.

Noisy Filter Got You Rattled?

Apart from the chugging sound you might hear if you fail to prime your mechanical filter, its operation should be fairly silent. Hearing a rattling or chattering noise from your filter suggests that the impeller isn't spinning properly. This may be due to physical damage to the impeller—such as a broken fin or bent shaft—or the impeller may not be seated correctly because of accumulated gunk on the impeller or in the compartment that houses it. If your impeller is broken or damaged, it's time to replace it. To prevent gunk buildup, these components should be brushed clean at regular intervals (such as during routine water changes).

Protein Skimmer Produces Flimsy Foam

The foam produced by your protein skimmer should be thick, brown, and dry. To get an idea of the correct color and consistency, think of the head of foam that appears on top of a root beer float. Once it reaches the collection cup, the foam should gradually collapse into a thick, dark-brown liquid. If, instead, your skimmer produces flimsy foam that collapses into a clear liquid, you're most likely not getting the right mixture of air bubbles and water in your skimmer chamber.

Check the Water Level

If your skimmer's foam production is poor, check the water height in your skimmer column to make sure it's at the optimum level recommended by the manufacturer. Adjusting the outflow of the skimmer up or down will change the water level in the skimmer column. Lowering the water level in the column often helps to improve the consistency of the foam produced.

Got Enough Air in There?

On the other hand, it may be that the water level is fine, but an insufficient amount of air is being introduced to the skimmer column. If you suspect this is the case, check the skimmer's air-intake hose and/or valve to make sure they're not clogged with a buildup of calcium. Soaking the clogged components in vinegar for a few hours will dissolve this buildup and help to get your skimmer foaming at peak efficiency again. If your skimmer employs an airstone to produce bubbles, poor foam production is a sign that its pores are getting clogged. It's time to buy a new one.

My Pump is Kaput!

Pumps, powerheads, and any hoses or pipes they might be connected to are the circulatory system of your aquarium, delivering aquarium water to various filtration components and providing vital water movement within the tank itself. And, just like your heart and blood vessels, your aquarium's circulatory system is vulnerable to clogging—only the clogging is usually caused by deposits of calcium, coralline algae, and other gunk instead of cholesterol.

Keep the Intake Free of Debris—and Snails

The slotted intakes of pumps and powerheads should be brushed routinely to keep them free of

Keep Your Neck Clean

As your protein skimmer skims away, it will gradually develop a layer of slimy brown gunk around the neck of the skimmer column. This buildup can lead to poor foam production and should be wiped away with a clean rag or paper towel every time you empty the skimmer's collection cup.

Your fish will not get their much-needed oxygen if a pump fails.

algae, uneaten food, fish waste, and other debris. Snails seem to be drawn to powerhead intakes like moths to a flame, so any powerhead located in a display tank that houses snails must be checked daily to make sure no mischievous mollusks have gotten stuck on the intake. If they are, simply unplug the powerhead and give the snails time to move along under their own power or pick them off the intake by hand and relocate them to a more suitable location.

The Vinegar Soak

To keep a pump or powerhead flowing freely, some simple preventive maintenance is in order. Every two months or so, depending on the level of coralline algae growth in your tank, remove the pump or powerhead from your system, place it in a clean bucket, and completely submerge it in a mixture of approximately one part white vinegar and four parts tap water. This will dissolve deposits of calcium and coralline algae. Allow it to soak for about a half hour, and then brush off any remaining deposits from the pump casing and components with a stiff-bristled toothbrush. Next, making sure the output is directed toward the side of the bucket, plug in the pump or powerhead and let it run for about 15 minutes to dislodge any deposits in the inner workings. Then, unplug the pump, pour out the vinegar/water mixture and refill the bucket with plain

A white vinegar soak is an easy solution to getting rid of the coralline algae on this heater.

wallet to buy a new one, try soaking the pump for an hour or so in undiluted white vinegar. Then, plug in the pump while it's still in the bucket to see whether or not it will kick in. If it does start, allow it to run for about 15 minutes and then perform a rinse cycle as described earlier before returning it to the tank. If the pump still doesn't work, all you've lost due to this added step is a little time and some cheap vinegar.

Keep Those Hoses Flowing

Hoses that have become coated on the inside with a layer of gunk have a decreased water output and put more strain on the pump, reducing its operational lifespan. Replacing hoses on a regular basis is an easy solution to this problem, but there's also a simple technique you can use to keep those hoses gunk-free when they are still in fairly good condition otherwise.

Take a section of twine or airline tubing that is several inches longer than the clogged-up hose and thread it through the hose until it emerges at the far end. You may need to attach the twine or tubing to a length of rigid wire to accomplish this. Next, tie one end of the twine or tubing to the handle of an aquarium brush that has a diameter just slightly larger than the inside diameter of the hose. Then, grab the other end of the twine or tubing

tap water to rinse off the vinegar. Plug the pump back in for a few minutes to rinse the pump's interior. Your pump will then be ready to return to service in your aquarium.

My Pump Stopped Working!

You've just finished a water change and plugged your equipment back in when you notice that water isn't being pumped back from your sump. Time to run to your local aquarium store for a new pump, right? Well, it might just be clogged. Don't give up on that pump too quickly! Before opening your and pull the brush through the hose. Repeat this process, running tap water through the hose after each pass of the brush, until the inside walls of the hose are completely clean.

Conquering Excessive Coralline Algae Buildup

The growth of pink and purple coralline algae is desirable in the saltwater aquarium. Not only are these algae very attractive, but their presence is also an indicator of good water quality. So, why would you need to control these algae if they're so beneficial? Well, it is possible to have too much of a good thing, especially when coralline algae start to form a thick coat on every submerged piece of equipment, including heaters, thermometers, powerheads, overflow chambers, filter intakes and returns, and, of course, the glass or acrylic panes of your aquarium.

Fortunately, it's easy to keep equipment surfaces clean of coralline algae provided you don't let it grow too thick before you decide to take action. For cleaning glass or acrylic panes, the standard algae magnet usually won't suffice when it comes to combating coralline (though daily use of an algae magnet will help prevent the coralline from establishing a foothold on the panes in the first place). A rigid, single-edge razor blade, on the other hand, will make quick work of coralline on glass. Do not use a razor blade on acrylic, however, as it

will scratch the surface. Use a scraper designed specifically for acrylic instead.

Stay One Step Ahead of Salt Creep

We briefly touched upon salt creep in Chapter 3, but since this phenomenon presents an ongoing maintenance challenge, it bears repeating here. If you recall, salt creep is the crusty buildup of salt on aquarium components that are positioned close to the water surface, where they are exposed to saltwater spray. The more turbulence at the water surface, the more salt creep will accumulate on nearby components and equipment. Cords from heaters and powerheads, glass covers, lighting

Versatile Vinegar

Coralline-algae-encrusted equipment that can be removed from the aquarium—heaters, thermometers, filter intakes, etc.—can be cleaned using our old friend white vinegar. Either soak the component in a bowl of vinegar or scrub it clean with a vinegar-soaked rag or sponge. Tough deposits usually require a combination of soaking and scrubbing.

hoods, and hang-on-tank filters and protein skimmers are especially vulnerable to salt creep buildup.

Apart from being messy and unpleasant to look at, salt creep can pose a serious safety hazard if it is allowed to work its way down a power cord into an electrical socket. Controlling salt creep is a simple matter of wiping down vulnerable surfaces with a moistened cloth on a frequent basis. To clean power cords, first unplug the device and then, starting where the cord meets the plug, run a slightly damp cloth along the length of cord until you reach the electrical device. Follow the damp cloth with a dry towel to make sure the cord is completely dry before plugging it back in.

The Water Level in My Sump Won't Equalize

A sump—a separate tank of water located below the main display tank—can be incorporated into an aquarium system's design for a variety of reasons. For example, sumps are very commonly used as the location for a wet/dry filter, protein skimmer, or refugium. Hobbyists hooking up a sump for the first time often go through a particularly frustrating experience—they can't seem to get the water level in the sump to equalize. That is, the rate at which water flows down to the sump is either slower or faster than the rate at which it gets pumped back to the main tank. Several factors can be involved here.

Wrong-Size Pump

If the water pump you place in the sump is designed to pump more gallons of water per hour than your overflow box is capable of delivering to the sump, the water level in your sump will quickly fall and the pump will end up sitting high and dry. This is a bad scenario because a submersible pump will soon burn out if it's allowed to run dry. On the other hand, if the pump can't keep pace with the amount of water flowing down from the aquarium, the water level in the sump will keep rising until it eventually spills onto the floor.

Most aquarium dealers bundle wet-dry filters with the right-sized pump, taking the guesswork out of the situation. If your dealer doesn't do this, he or she should still be able to recommend the right pump for your system.

Simple Adjustments Are Needed

What happens if you know you've got the right sized pump but you're still having problems equalizing the water level in your sump? In this case, you need to look at the other half of the equation—the overflow.

The most common method for delivering water from an aquarium to a sump is through an overflow box of some kind. Typically, an overflow consists of two chambers—one positioned inside the tank and one that hangs off the back of the tank. The inside chamber is slotted to allow

aquarium water to flow in. A U-shaped siphon tube draws water from the inside chamber to the outside chamber where it is carried through a flexible tube down into the sump.

The inside chamber of the overflow is usually designed so that the level of the slots in the water can be adjusted, thereby decreasing or increasing the amount of water flowing into the overflow box and down to the sump. If the water level in the sump keeps rising, you simply raise up the inside chamber in small increments until you achieve the desired balance. The opposite action—lowering the inside chamber in the tank—will raise the water level in the sump. This can be a painstaking process, but your patience will pay off.

Clogged Components

In some cases, a sump system that has been in operation for a long period loses equilibrium. Clogged components are usually the culprit here. It may be that the pump is clogged with calcium buildup or that the return hose is

A Bubble in the Siphon Tube

A large air bubble in the U-shaped siphon tube can also slow the rate of water flowing through the overflow to the sump, thereby lowering the water level in the sump. Often, rapidly raising and lowering the siphon tube, taking care not to break the siphon, will cause the trapped air to flow out of the tube. If that doesn't work, you may need to break and restart the siphon.

narrowed with gunk. Either way, pumping capacity will be diminished, causing the water level in the sump to rise.

Or, it may be that the prefilter sponge in the overflow is clogged with debris or that hair algae is blocking the slots on the overflow chamber or plugging the siphon tube. In these situations, water flow through the overflow box will be reduced, causing the water level in the sump to fall. The message here is that it's very important to keep all of the components of your sump system clean so that the water continues to flow as it should.

Defeating Water-Movement Dead Spots

Wave action, tides, and ever-shifting currents keep the water around natural coral reefs in constant motion, and, for the health of the livestock, you must replicate these conditions, to the extent possible, in your aquarium system.

Water movement serves many important purposes in the aquarium:

- keeping debris suspended in the water column so that it can be captured and removed by the mechanical filter
- preventing detritus from settling on the rockwork

- keeping fish healthier since they must work to swim against the varying currents
- helping oxygenate the water, which is vital to the health of livestock and the process of nitrification

Mother Nature Does It Best

While the water movement on the natural coral reefs tends to be very turbulent and non-linear (i.e., random and multidirectional), it can be very challenging to recreate this natural effect in the aquarium when all you have to work with are manmade sources of linear water movement— powerheads, filter returns, etc. As a result, dead spots, or areas of little or no water movement, can develop in your tank.

Spotting Water-Movement Dead Spots

How can you identify water-movement dead spots? You can usually recognize them by the accumulation of detritus on the rockwork in a particular area. Also, as explained in Chapter 5, cyanobacteria and flatworms tend to prosper in areas of minimal water flow, so these problems can be a tip-off, as well.

Get Creative With Currents

Preventing or eliminating water-movement dead spots takes some creative use of the linear currents we have at our disposal. Powerheads can be positioned at various locations in the tank, say, one near the surface of the water at the front of the tank with its output flowing in one direction while another could be placed near the bottom at the rear of the tank to create a current flowing in the opposite direction. You can also direct the flow of two or more powerheads so that they intersect one another or reflect off of the aquarium glass to create the desired non-linear, turbulent water movement. Don't forget that the return hose from your sump or a canister filter is a good source of water movement, too.

Many Ways to Make Waves

A great way to maximize water movement is to use oscillating powerheads, which are designed to rotate back and forth, directing flow to a greater portion of the tank. A similar effect can be achieved by attaching a rotating deflector to the output of a powerhead or your sump return.

Also, there's a newer device on the market, called a switching current water director (SCWD), that is designed to take the water flow from a pump or powerhead and switch it between two different outputs. The pressure produced by the pump determines how fast the SCWD switches from one output to the other (the stronger the pump, the faster the device switches).

Yet another way to get the water moving is through the use of a wave-maker system, which essentially consists of an electronic timer and multiple powerheads (either standard or oscillating). The timer turns the powerheads on and off in an alternating fashion, which frequently changes the direction of current in the tank, creating a wave-like effect.

Cyanobacteria will appear in your tank if you do not take care of water-movement dead spots.

Chapter 7

Fish Health

Problems Solved

Watching helplessly as a beloved fish—worse yet, a whole tank full of beloved fish—gets sick and dies is a heartbreaking experience for even the most seasoned saltwater aquarist. That's why it's so important to take a proactive approach to your fish's health and to take immediate action when disease symptoms appear.

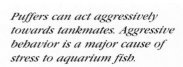

Stress Kills!

Just as people are more prone to illness when they're under stress, so too are the fish in our care. Chronic stress weakens a fish's immune system, leaving it vulnerable to illness and infections that it could easily fight off otherwise.

So, what stresses out a fish? For starters, there's the epic journey wild-caught specimens must endure from the time they're captured on the reef to the point that they finally arrive in the hobbyist's aquarium. Given the less-than-ideal conditions under which they're kept and the frequent re-acclimation they must go through, it should come as no surprise that a newly introduced fish is usually highly stressed and especially vulnerable to illness. Other stressors might include

Puffers can act aggressively towards tankmates. Aggressive behavior is a major cause of stress to aquarium fish.

poor water quality, fluctuating water parameters, poor diet, overcrowding, constant squabbling with tankmates, excessive human activity in the vicinity of the tank, and many other factors.

Who Salted My Fish?

One of the most common fish ailments aquarists encounter is *Cryptocaryon irritans*, better known as saltwater ich. Caused by a parasitic protozoan, this disease appears as small white specks on the bodies of fish, creating the appearance that the fish has been sprinkled with salt. The infected fish may also rub and scrape its body against the substrate or rockwork in an effort to rid itself of the irritant.

A case of *Cryptocaryon irritans* isn't an automatic death sentence but can be fatal in severe cases or to a fish

Quarantine—Your First Line of Defense

In Chapter 2, we discussed the importance of quarantining new specimens before introducing them to your aquarium. Quarantining is the best thing you can do to protect your community of fishes from disease. The modest investment and minimal inconvenience associated with quarantining is nothing compared to the cost and hassle of losing a tank full of valuable fish.

that is malnourished or otherwise stressed. And, keep in mind that if the infected specimen has already been introduced to your display tank, you must assume all the other fish in your system have been infected and treat them all accordingly.

A Day in the Life Cycle

Because of its multistage life cycle, *Cryptocaryon irritans* can be a challenge to eradicate once it's introduced to an aquarium. Here's how it works:

In the first stage (depending on where in the cycle you choose to begin), the parasite is attached to and feeding on a host fish. The parasite then detaches from its host, drops to the bottom of the tank, and forms a cyst. While encysted, the parasite multiplies until there are hundreds of new parasites inside the cyst. This stage can last up to a month (which explains why fish that are thought to be cured of this disease are often reinfected, to the aquarist's dismay). The parasites then hatch out of the cyst in a free-swimming form, searching for a host fish. If a host is not found within a day or two, they die.

Careful With Copper!

Copper-based medications have long been used with good results in combating *Cryptocaryon irritans* and other parasitic infections, but these products must be used with caution. Although it is safe to use copper in a true fish-only system (with no invertebrates present—including those found on live rock), copper will bond to calcium-based materials, such as your rocks and substrate, so it's preferable to transfer the infected fish to a separate, bare-bottomed tank for treatment.

As with any medication, proper dosage is critical when administering copper. Use too much, and you risk killing all of your fish. Use too little, and your treatment won't be therapeutic. Follow the manufacturer's dosing recommendations to the letter while monitoring the copper level with a high-quality test kit. Make sure your test

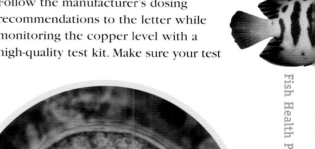

A magnified view of a saltwater ich organism, Cryptocaryon irritans.

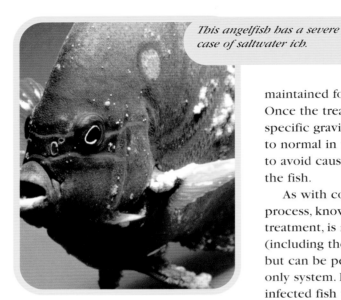

This angelfish has a severe case of saltwater ich.

RO/DI-purified fresh water. This lower specific gravity should be maintained for at least four weeks. Once the treatment is finished, the specific gravity should be raised back to normal in the same gradual manner to avoid causing osmotic shock to the fish.

As with copper treatments, this process, known as a hyposalinity treatment, is not safe for invertebrates (including those encrusting live rock) but can be performed in a true fish-only system. Better yet, transfer the infected fish to your quarantine tank for treatment, filling the tank halfway with water from your display tank and then gradually diluting it with purified fresh water until you've reached the desired specific gravity.

kit is appropriate for measuring the form of copper you're using, as well. Some kits are formulated for testing only chelated copper, while others test only ionic copper. Also, keep in mind that certain fishes, such as dragonets, puffers, lionfishes, and clownfishes, are sensitive to copper and should not be treated with copper-based medications at all.

Hyposalinity Treatment

As a safer alternative to copper and other medications, *Cryptocaryon irritans* can be treated by lowering the specific gravity of your aquarium water into the range of 1.010 to 1.012—a level that can be tolerated by the fish but not by the parasites. This change should be made over the course of several days by removing small amounts of salt water and replacing them with

Remove the Hosts, Destroy the Parasites

Removing all the fish from a system infected with *Cryptocaryon irritans* for a minimum of four weeks (six weeks is even better) effectively breaks the vicious cycle. Remember, once this parasite reaches the free-swimming stage, it needs to find a host quickly or it will die. No hosts equals no more parasites.

Virulent Velvet

Amyloodinium ocellatum, or marine velvet, is another common fish ailment caused by a parasite—in this case, a type of dinoflagellate (a one-celled organism that uses a whip-like flagellum to move around). However, this disease is much more infectious and deadly than *Cryptocaryon irritans*. If symptoms of this disease are observed, prompt action must be taken to save the infected specimen as well as to prevent the spread of the parasite to all the other fish in your system. Again, if the infected fish is in your display tank, you should treat all of your fish as if they are infected.

Symptoms of *Amyloodinium ocellatum* include gasping or rapid breathing, rubbing or scraping against the rockwork or substrate, and the presence of a velvety or powdery coating on the body of the fish.

A Familiar Life Cycle

The life cycle of *Amyloodinium ocellatum* is similar to that of Cryptocaryon irritans. The feeding form of the parasite attaches to the fish using thin, root-like structures. When it matures, it detaches from the host fish and forms a cyst, which settles to the substrate and begins to divide internally. When the cyst hatches, over 200 free-swimming parasites emerge and begin searching for a host fish. If no host is found within several days, the parasites will die. The entire life cycle can take anywhere from a week to three weeks.

To the QT ASAP!

Specimens infected with *Amyloodinium ocellatum* should be moved to the quarantine tank immediately for treatment. As with treating saltwater ich, copper is the most common weapon of choice for combating *Amyloodinium ocellatum*, and all the same warnings and precautions apply to its use. Hyposalinity treatments are also commonly recommended for controlling this parasite. And, as you've probably figured out already, because

SMALL FRY

Good Things Come to Those Who Wait

A four-week quarantine period for new specimens can seem like an eternity to kids who are eager to see a bustling aquarium filled with colorful fish. Tell your kids that you're excited about stocking the tank, too, but that you want to do it right the first time so you don't end up with a bunch of sick or dying fish on your hands. To help keep their minds off the wait and to get them involved in the process, ask them to report on the condition of the fish in quarantine every day.

the free-swimming stage of this parasite must find a host fish in fairly short order, removing all of the fish from the infected system for at least four weeks is the best way to eradicate *Amyloodinium ocellatum* in your display tank and to prevent reinfection.

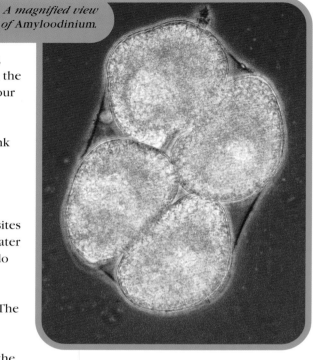

A magnified view of Amyloodinium.

The Freshwater Dip

An excellent technique for ridding fish of attached parasites is giving them a brief freshwater dip. In fact, many hobbyists do this as a precaution with all newly purchased fish before placing them in quarantine. The freshwater dip is a simple technique that can pay huge dividends when it comes to the health of your fishes.

All the equipment you'll need for this method is a clean plastic or glass container that is deep enough so the fish can be fully submerged. A large bowl or small bucket will usually suffice. Fill the container with purified, aerated tap water of the same temperature and pH as the water in your system. Next, place the fish in the container for approximately five minutes, watching it closely throughout the process. Remove the fish from the container and return it to salt water immediately if it begins to show signs of distress. To prevent the fish from jumping out, place a net or other obstruction over the container. After five minutes, you can return the fish to the aquarium.

I Need This Like a Hole in the Head!

If you notice that one of your fish is experiencing tissue loss or developing ulcers, pits, or holes on its head and along its lateral line (the series of sensory pores that forms a line on the sides of fish), you're probably dealing with a case of head and lateral line erosion (HLLE), also known as hole-in-the-head disease. While this disease progresses very slowly and is fatal only in advanced cases, it can cause permanent, ugly scarring on affected specimens.

A Disease of Unknown Origin

Experts can't seem to agree on the exact cause of HLLE. Some suggest the cause is related to nutrition, such as some important element or vitamin missing from the fish's diet. Others speculate that the problem could be environmental in nature, such as excessive dissolved pollutants, the accidental introduction of household chemicals, stray voltage produced by submersed powerheads or heaters, or even the use of activated carbon for chemical filtration. Still others point to a combination of nutritional and environmental factors.

This tang, Zebrasoma *sp., has advanced HLLE.*

Better Care Might Be the Cure

So, if no one is absolutely certain what causes HLLE, how do you go about preventing or curing it? Well, many aquarists have noted improvement in specimens with this condition (or at least that the symptoms stopped getting worse) after making significant changes to both their living conditions and diet.

In one case, for example, significant improvement was seen after a yellow tang *Zebrasoma flavescens* with HLLE was given a major nutritional and environmental upgrade. The tang was moved from a crowded, undersized, fish-only tank with a high nitrate level to a much larger, lightly stocked reef system with exceptional water quality. At the same time, dried nori (the stuff they use to wrap sushi) and red marine algae soaked in a vitamin supplement were added to its menu. Prior to that, its greens consisted mostly of romaine lettuce and spinach. The result was that the HLLE symptoms stopped advancing, many (but not all) of the pits and ulcers filled back in with tissue, and the specimen, which had faded in color, regained its vibrant canary-yellow coloration. So, what caused the improvement? Better diet? Better environmental conditions? Both? Some other unrelated factor? It's impossible to say for sure. But one thing's certain—there's no downside to giving your fish the best possible nutrition and water conditions.

Medication

I See Eye Problems!

A variety of eye problems can afflict marine fishes, the most common being cloudy eyes and bulging eyes. There are numerous possible causes for these conditions, such as physical injury, bacterial infection, vitamin deficiency, and poor water quality.

Whenever an eye problem is observed, check all water parameters to make sure your water quality is impeccable and evaluate the diet you're offering to ensure that it's sufficiently varied and nutritious.

Cloudy Eyes

Cloudy eyes most commonly develop as a result of injury to the eye or a bacterial infection. Newly introduced fish that are behaving skittishly and fish that are being constantly badgered by tankmates often scrape their eyes on rocks while dashing around the tank. Once the skittish fish has had a chance to acclimate or is no longer being harassed—and provided your water quality is exceptional—the cloudiness will usually clear up with time.

If the cloudiness persists, the problem is probably bacterial, and it may be necessary to move the fish to your quarantine tank for treatment with antibiotics. Follow the dosing instructions carefully, and be sure to administer the full recommended course of treatment. Never treat your display tank with antibiotics, as this can wipe out the beneficial bacteria that make up your biological filter. Some antibiotic products claim that they will not harm your biological filter, but why risk it? Besides, it takes less medication to treat a small quarantine tank than it does to

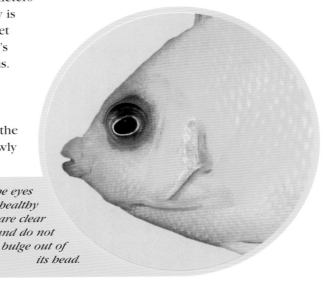

The eyes of a healthy fish are clear and do not bulge out of its head.

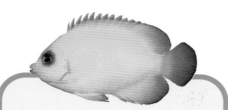

How Does a Freshwater Dip Kill parasites?

The freshwater dip is just an extreme form of the hyposalinity treatment. Because water flows from areas of lower salt concentration to areas of higher salt concentration (remember the concept of osmosis described in Chapter 3?), the fresh water in the container will keep flowing into the delicate bodies of the tiny parasites (where the salt concentration is higher) until they burst like a balloon filled with too much air. Fish, on the other hand, are able to tolerate being immersed in fresh water for much longer than the parasites can, so they typically come through the treatment unharmed.

treat a larger display tank, which helps minimize the cost of treatment.

Bulging Eyes

In some cases, a fish's eye or eyes will actually bulge right out of its head, as if they've been pumped full of air. This condition, known as exophthalmia, or pop-eye, is usually treatable but can result in the loss of the affected eye or eyes or the death of the specimen. As with cloudy eyes, exophthalmia is most commonly caused by injury to the eye or a bacterial infection. When injury is the cause, it's typical for only one eye to be affected, whereas a bacterial infection usually affects both eyes.

If only one eye is bulging, it's a good idea to shift the fish into quarantine where it can recuperate in isolation. To help bring down the swelling, you can try the old time-tested method of adding epsom salts to the quarantine tank at a rate of one teaspoon to every 10 gallons (40 liters) of water. If both eyes are affected, you'll need to quarantine and medicate the fish with antibiotics.

I've Heard of Cauliflower Ear, but This is Ridiculous!

If you spot lumpy, wart-like growths on one of your fishes, it's probably infected with *Lymphocystis*, or cauliflower disease. The disease earned this unusual name because the white, warty growths somewhat resemble the vegetable. The growths most commonly appear on the edges of fins, but they can appear elsewhere on the body as well, including the mouth and gills.

Lymphocystis is caused by a virus that affects the connective tissue. Because it is contagious, any infected specimen should be moved into quarantine until symptoms clear up completely. Maintaining excellent water quality and providing a nutritious, varied diet will help your fish fight off this disease.

Chapter 8

What's Next?

Hopefully the tips and suggestions in this book will help you overcome the challenges that go hand in hand with saltwater aquariums and give you the confidence you need to move on to even greater things in this wonderful hobby. But where can you go from here?

From Generalist to Specialist

Perhaps you'd like to narrow your focus from keeping a diverse community of bread-and-butter species to specializing in a particular species or a group of closely related fishes that really appeals to you. For instance, you might want to set up a tank specifically to house a group of jawfish, so that you can discover more about their fascinating behaviors. Or, maybe you'd like to keep more challenging fish, such as seahorses. Or, how about a specimen tank containing a single, exotic animal, such as a lionfish or frogfish. The sky (sea?) is truly the limit when it comes to your options here.

Breeding

Unlike the freshwater aquarium hobby, where many of the commonly sold species can be bred in captivity relatively easily, only a handful of marine fishes are routinely bred by hobbyists. That means plenty of opportunities exist for experimentation and breakthroughs in the area of breeding. Who knows? You could be the first hobbyist to breed a species that has never successfully reproduced in the aquarium before!

Or, if you'd prefer to follow a better-worn path, you might want to try your hand with a fish that has a proven record of successful captive breeding, such as clownfishes or cardinalfishes.

In the same fish family as lionfish (Scorpaenidae), scorpionfish are generally sedentary and have, like lions, venomous spines.

The Reef Aquarium

This book focuses mostly on fish-only systems—the logical entry point for the saltwater aquarium hobby. However, many hobbyists who first get their feet wet by keeping marine fishes are eventually drawn to keeping corals and other invertebrates in a reef aquarium. What will you need to know in order to succeed with a reef tank? Everything you've already learned still applies, but some additional considerations make reef systems even more challenging.

Fish Are No Longer the Focus

In a reef tank, the emphasis is on the corals and other invertebrates, not so much on the fish. The population of fish is kept small, specimens are chosen based on their compatibility with the invertebrates, and heavy polluters (large fishes that produce a lot of waste) are kept out.

Light Equals Life

Whereas lighting in a fish-only system serves primarily to illuminate the fish for the enjoyment of the hobbyist, lighting in a reef system is critical to the survival of the corals and other invertebrates. Most aquarium corals are photosynthetic. That is, they have symbiotic algae, called zooxanthellae, living in their tissues. The zooxanthellae need light of the correct intensity and spectral qualities to photosynthesize the nutrients they need. They also share these nutrients with their invertebrate hosts, which is what makes it possible for corals to survive in the nutrient-poor—but sun-drenched—waters around coral reefs.

Water Quality Is Even More Critical

Exceptional water quality is very important in a fish-only system, but reef invertebrates are even more demanding when it comes to water quality. For example, while fish can tolerate relatively high nitrate levels, the nitrate in a reef system must be kept as close to zero as possible. In addition, whereas hardier fish species can survive maintenance missteps that result in fluctuating water parameters—pH, temperature, etc.—such errors often prove deadly to corals.

Additives Enter the Scene

In the fish-only system, all the elements the fishes need to thrive are found in

You're on Your Own, Kid!

Kids, imagine if the minute you were born, you were swept away by ocean currents, drifted with the plankton, eventually settled far, far from home, and never even saw your parents. That's what life is like for most baby reef fishes!

the sea-salt mix and are sufficiently replenished through regular water changes. Your salt mix has all the ingredients for healthy corals in a reef system as well, but they tend to use up calcium and buffering compounds faster than they can be replaced through water changes. Therefore, it's necessary to supplement these elements in a reef system.

What? More Problems?

As you've probably concluded already, whether you choose to specialize in a certain species, breed your favorite fish, or shift your focus to reef invertebrates, you'll no doubt be faced with a completely new set of problems and challenges. But don't let that discourage you! There are solutions to all those problems, too. What are those solutions? Well, that's a subject for a different book.

Resources

Magazine

Tropical Fish Hobbyist
1 TFH Plaza
3rd & Union Avenues
Neptune City, NJ 07753
E-mail: info@tfh.com
www.tfhmagazine.com

Internet Resources

Aquaria Central
www.aquariacentral.com

Aquarium Hobbyist
www.aquariumhobbyist.com

Fish Geeks
www.fishgeeks.com

Reef Central
www.reefcentral.com

Tropical Resources
www.tropicalresources.net

Wet Web Media
www.wetwebmedia.com

A World of Fish
www.aworldoffish.com

Books

Boruchowitz, David E. *Setup and Care of Saltwater Aquariums.* TFH Publications, Inc.

Brightwell, CR. *Marine Chemistry.* TFH Publications, Inc.

Fatherree, James W. *The Super Simple Guide to Corals.* TFH Publications, Inc.

Fenner, Robert M. *The Conscientious Marine Aquarist.* Microcosm/TFH Publications, Inc.

Kurtz, Jeffrey. *The Simple Guide to Marine Aquariums.* TFH Publications, Inc.

Kurtz, Jeffrey. *The Simple Guide to Mini-Reef Aquariums.* TFH Publications, Inc.

Michael, Scott W. *Adventurous Aquarist Guide™: The 101 Best Saltwater Fishes.* Microcosm/TFH Publications, Inc.

Wittenrich, Matthew L. *The Complete Illustrated Breeder's Guide to Marine Aquarium Fishes.* Microcosm/TFH Publications, Inc.

Index

Saltwater Aquarium Problem Solver

Dedication

To my wonderful wife, Melissa, and beloved children, Aidan and Hannah.

About the Author

Jeff Kurtz is a freelance writer and editor living in Toledo, Ohio. Jeff has been involved in the aquarium hobby for over 25 years and is a regular contributor to *Tropical Fish Hobbyist* Magazine. He is also the author of *The Simple Guide to Marine Aquariums* and *The Simple Guide to Mini-Reef Aquariums*.

Photo Credits

REACH OUT. ACT. RESPOND.
Go to AnimalPlanet.com/ROAR and find out how you can be a voice for animals everywhere!

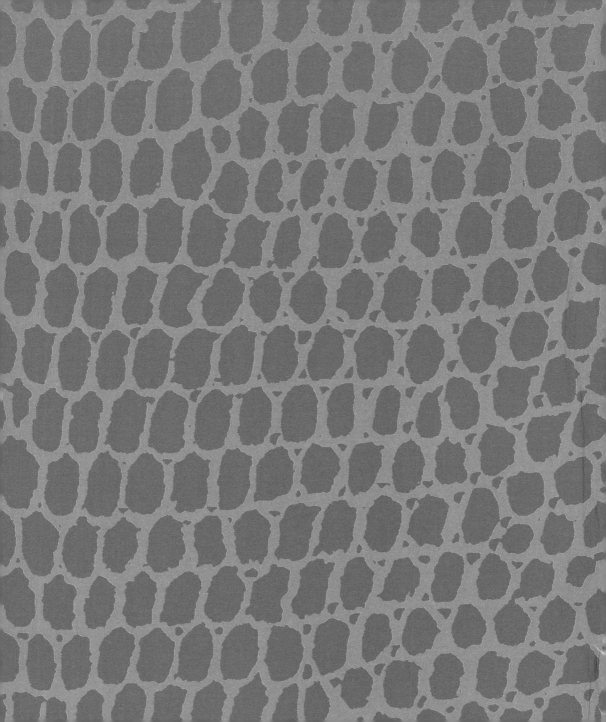